Basic HTML

Teacher Resources

PAYNE-GALLWAY
PUBLISHERS LTD

Basic HTML Teacher Resources

Published by
Payne-Gallway Publishers Limited
26-28 Northgate Street
Ipswich IP1 3DB
Tel 01473 251097

First edition 2004

10 09 08 07 06 05
10 9 8 7 6 5 4 3 2

10-digit ISBN: 1 904467 44 X
13-digit ISBN: 978 1 904467 44 1

You can order online at
www.payne-gallway.co.uk

E-mail: orders@payne-gallway.co.uk

Printed and Bound by
Pear Tree Press Ltd, Stevenage Herts, England

Basic HTML Teacher Resources

Preface

This document contains sixteen worksheets divided into two sections, Series A and Series B. Each series has one worksheet for each chapter in '*Basic HTML*'. The worksheets are intended to provide extra practice in techniques already learned, and to occupy faster students while others in a group catch up.

There is some advice given for each worksheet on anything you will need to prepare or might want to point out to the students before they attempt the exercise.
Each Worksheet A can be completed away from the computer. The students will need to use a computer with Internet access to complete each Worksheet B.

We hope you will find these exercises useful and fun for the students to complete. A helpful HTML reference sheet is included for pupils at the end of Series A. Answers to all exercises can be found at the end of each series. Finally you will find a set of answer sheets. These are provided so that only one colour copy of the worksheets needs to be printed out (and laminated if necessary), allowing pupils to fill in their answers on the black and white answer sheet instead. The answer sheets are mostly only one page long, so using them will save plenty of paper and toner.

Payne-Gallway Publishers Ltd 2004

Basic HTML

Teacher Resources

Series A

Basic HTML Teacher Resources
Worksheet 1A – HTML and the Internet
Teacher's notes

Topics covered in this worksheet

- Uses of web sites on the Internet
- Differences between **browsers** and **editors**
- Advantages of writing HTML (rather than having a program create it automatically)

This worksheet is intended for additional practice or assessment after Chapter 1 of *Basic HTML* has been completed. The students should be provided with a copy of *Basic HTML* and a printout of the worksheet, whilst they work through the tasks away from the computer.

This worksheet can be used towards covering Activity 1 in Unit 9 of QCA Year 8 Schemes of Work.

Note: Students can do everything in this worksheet and the book *Basic HTML* using any modern Operating System. The only software requirements are a browser, a plain text editor, a simple image editor and an FTP client. The following table shows recommended software for the creation of web sites using *Basic HTML*. All of this software is either bundled with the Operating System or free to download.

System	Microsoft Windows	Apple Macintosh	Linux (UNIX)
Browser	Microsoft Internet Explorer, Netscape or Opera	Microsoft Internet Explorer or Netscape	Netscape, Mozilla, Opera, Galeon or Konqueror
Text Editor	Microsoft Notepad	Simple Text	Gedit or Kedit
Image Editor	Microsoft Paint		GIMP, xv or ee
FTP client	FileZilla FTP (see *Basic HTML* (2nd ed.) Page 60)		ftp, gftp, kftp or xftp
Comments	Any FTP client can be used to upload web sites to the Internet. FileZilla FTP is only suggested because it is easy to use.	The screenshots used in this pack and in *Basic HTML* were created in Windows so they will not be quite the same as a Mac or Linux system. Some applications will be in different menus and, for example, methods such as creating a new folder will not be the same as illustrated.	

In the above table, underlined software is usually installed by default on your system.

Basic HTML
Worksheet 1A – HTML and the Internet

Student Name:________________________ **Date:**__________________

1. What does HTML stand for?

____

2. Write down four things that a web site could be used for:

   a) ____

   b) ____

   c) ____

   d) ____

3. Look at the two screenshots below.

Figure 1.1

Figure 1.2

Which is a browser and which is an editor?

a) ________________

b) ________________

4. Is Notepad

   a) a browser ☐

   b) an editor ☐

   c) a spreadsheet ☐

5. Name two of your favourite web sites and write what it is that you like about them.

   a) ____

   ____

   b) ____

   ____

6. Who can look at a web site on the Internet?

a) Only people in your school ☐

b) Only people in your country ☐

c) Only people in Europe or America ☐

d) Anyone in the world ☐

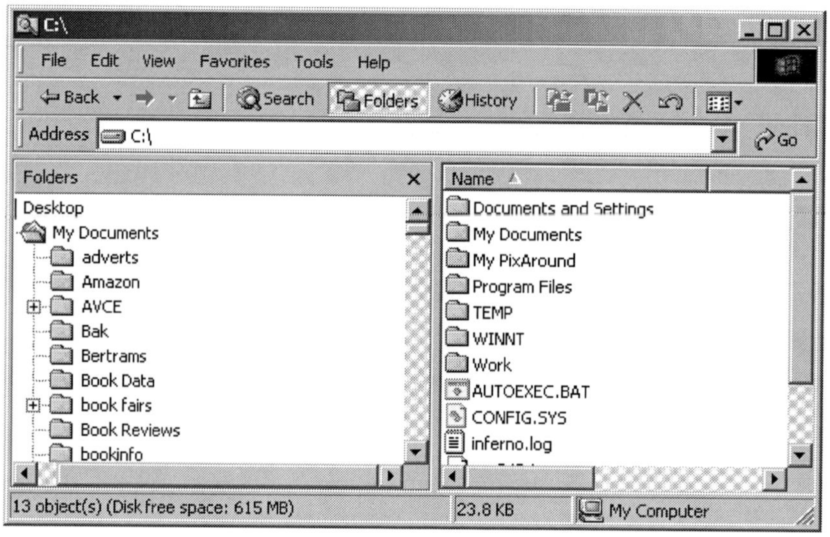

Figure 1.3

7. Look at Figure 1.3. Write down how you would make a new folder on drive C.

____

____

____

8. Look at these two screenshots.

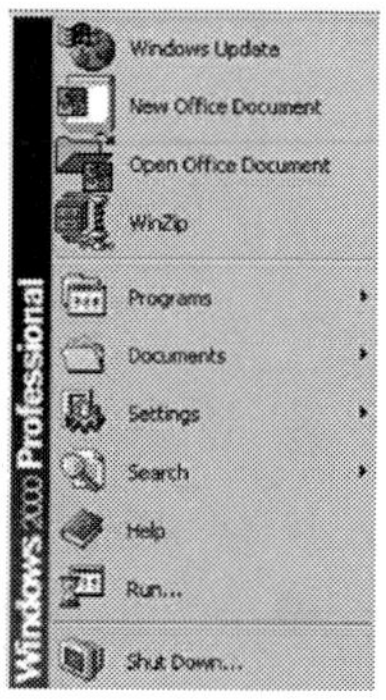

a.

Figure 1.4

Which is the **Start Menu** and which is the **taskbar**?

a) ____________________

b) ____________________

b.

Figure 1.5

9. How would you open a browser, such as Internet Explorer, from the **Start** menu?

____

____

10. If a company is making a very complicated web site, they will use special design programs to create the HTML code. For smaller web sites, it is often best to write all of the HTML code yourself, without a special program.

Tick the correct statements on this list.

a) Other programs often put extra code in that you don't need. This means your web site might take longer to load.

b) You learn a lot more by writing the code yourself.

c) You can't use as many extra features, like animation, graphics and sound if you write it yourself.

d) It takes longer to write the code.

11. What sort of things could make a web page really stand out?

____

____

____

Basic HTML Teacher Resources
Worksheet 2A – Writing HTML
Teacher's notes

Topics covered in this worksheet

- Start tags and end tags
- Viewing web pages in a browser
- Adding paragraphs
- The break tag `<BR>`
- Using parameters and values to extend the functions of HTML tags

This worksheet is intended for additional practice or assessment after Chapter 2 of *Basic HTML* has been completed. The students should be provided with a copy of *Basic HTML* and a printout of the worksheet, whilst they work through the tasks away from the computer. Worksheets / Answer sheets should be clearly named so that they can be marked for the answers to the questions.

Basic HTML
Worksheet 2A – Writing HTML

Student Name:________________________ **Date:**____________________

1. a) Which start tag would you use to begin an HTML document? _______

   b) Which end tag marks the last line of an HTML document? _______

2. Will the **</P>** tag start a paragraph or end a paragraph?

   ____

3. This code will make the word **hello** appear on the left-hand side of the screen.

```
<P ALIGN=LEFT>Hello</P>
```

   Which part of the code is a **parameter**? ________________________

   What **value** does this parameter have? ________________________

4. This is part of the code for somebody's first HTML document.

```
<TITLE>My First Web Page</TITLE>
```

   They view their page in a browser. On Figure 2.1, draw a box around the text which is produced by the `<TITLE>` tags.

Figure 2.1

5. If you make some changes to your code, which button must you press in the browser?

   ____

6. How should you spell the parameter for the <P> tag so that the paragraph will appear in the middle of the page?

   a) CENTER ☐

   b) CENTRE ☐

   c) SENTER ☐

7. Look at the code in Figure 2.2, and then at the browser in Figure 2.3.

```
<HTML>
  <HEAD>
     <TITLE>Danny's Delightful Donuts</TITLE>
  </HEAD>
  <BODY>
    <P ALIGN=CENTER>
      Drop dead gorgeous nuggets of Finest Flour,
      Fried to a Golden Brown and Dusted with Demerara Sugar
      then rolled in Technicolor Hundreds and Thousands.
      Your mouth will love you forever!
    </P>
  </BODY>
</HTML>
```

Figure 2.2

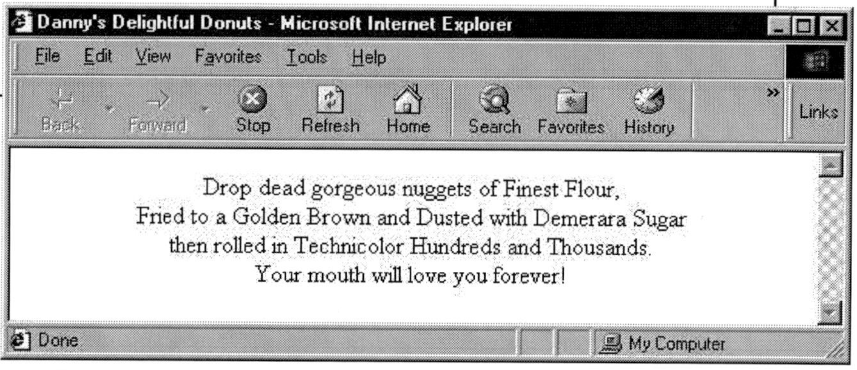

Figure 2.3

   Which type of tag does Danny need to add so that the page will look like Figure 2.3?

   ____

8. Write some of the tags (from your answer to Question 7) in the paragraph below to make the HTML code correct.

```
<P ALIGN=CENTER>
  Drop dead gorgeous nuggets of Finest Flour,
  Fried to a Golden Brown and Dusted with Demerara Sugar
  then rolled in Technicolor Hundreds and Thousands.
  Your mouth will love you forever!
</P>
```

9. What are the three main steps you should follow when writing and checking your web page?

   1) W _ _ _ _ the HTML code in an editor

   2) S _ _ _ the code as an HTML file

   3) View the page in a b _ _ _ _ _ _

Basic HTML Teacher Resources
Worksheet 3A – Writing HTML
Teacher's notes

Topics covered in this worksheet

- Image tags, `<IMG>`
- `HEIGHT` and `WIDTH` parameters
- Font sizes
- Extending the `<FONT>` tag

Images and fonts start to bring a web page to life. Students particularly enjoy personalising their web pages. This might be an opportunity to discuss what they would put on their own pages and the effects that different fonts have on visitors. For instance Times New Roman is very formal, whereas Comic sans MS is friendly, if rather overused. A session looking at fonts in a word processing program might be useful.

All modern computers have several 'system' fonts including Times New Roman, Arial and Courier New. It is usually best to keep to these or other widely used fonts.

Basic HTML
Worksheet 3A – Graphics and Fonts

Student Name:____________________ **Date:**________________

1. Which tag lets you add an image to a web page? ____________________

2. What are the two parameters used to set the size of an image?

   ____________________ and ____________________

3. In HTML, pictures and other objects aren't measured in centimetres.

   Instead, they are measured in units called ____________________

4. The `SRC` parameter is used to tell the browser where to look for the image file. Write down the entire tag that will add the image **my-picture.jpg** to your page, and set the width to 80 and the height to 100.

   ____

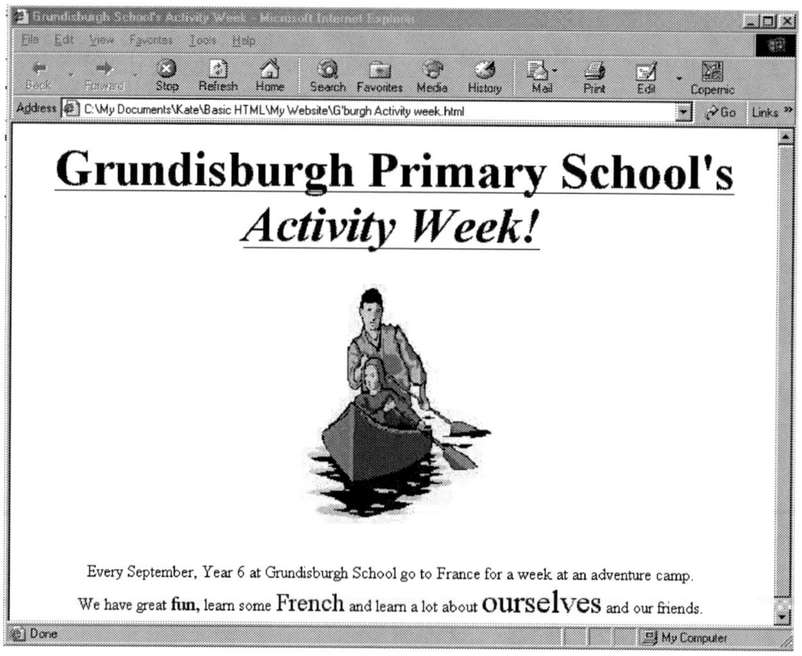

Figure 3.1

5. The picture in Figure 3.1 has a width of 250 pixels and a height of 200 pixels. What shape would it be if the height were 50 pixels and the width 300 pixels?

   a) Square ☐

   b) Portrait ☐

   c) Landscape ☐

Figure 3.2 is the code for the web page shown in Figure 3.1 with an extra paragraph at the foot of the page.

```
<HTML>
  <HEAD>
    <TITLE>Grundisburgh Primary School's Activity Week</TITLE>
  </HEAD>
  <BODY>
    <P ALIGN=CENTER>
      <FONT SIZE=7>
        <U><B>
          Grundisburgh Primary School's<BR>
          <I>Activity Week!</I>
        </B></U>
      </FONT>
    </P>
    <P ALIGN=CENTER>
       <IMG SRC="images/canoeing.jpg" WIDTH=200 HEIGHT=250>
    </P>
    <P ALIGN=CENTER>
      <FONT SIZE=1>
        Every September, Year 6 at Grundisburgh School go to France
        for a week at an adventure camp.<BR>
        We have great <FONT SIZE=3>fun</FONT>, learn some
        <FONT SIZE=4>French</FONT> and learn a lot about
        <FONT SIZE=5>ourselves</FONT> and our friends.
      </FONT>
    </P>
    <P ALIGN=RIGHT>
      <FONT COLOR=GRAY SIZE=2>Copyright 2002</FONT>
    </P>
  </BODY>
</HTML>
```

Figure 3.2

6. What are the smallest and largest font sizes used in Figure 3.2?

   Smallest ______________ Largest ______________

7. What are the smallest and largest font sizes allowed in HTML?

   Smallest ______________ Largest ______________

8. Write the start tags and end tags for these text styles.

   a) Underlined _______ _______

   b) Bold _______ _______

   c) Italic _______ _______

9. Which parameter for the `<FONT>` tag lets you choose a particular font, like **Arial** or **Times New Roman**?

   ____

10. Write the tags that would style the word **hello** to become bold, size 4 and **Comic Sans MS**.

    ____

Basic HTML Teacher Resources
Worksheet 4A – Colours and hyperlinks
Teacher's notes

Topics covered in this worksheet

- Background colour
- Font colour
- Preset colours
- Hexadecimal numbers
- Red, green and blue hexadecimal colour pairs
- Hyperlink tags

Preset colours allow students to start using colour without the terror of trying to work out hexadecimal. If hexadecimal is introduced as counting in sixteens, rather than tens in decimal, it can be an easier concept. Students should be encouraged to set up an html file to practise hexadecimal colours. A few short sessions with such a file will usually clarify the mysteries of colour.

It is a good idea to reiterate that hyperlinks are needed to navigate from page to page in a web site and also emphasise that if students take visitors to a page, they must also have a link to let them out again!

Basic HTML
Worksheet 4A – Colours and Hyperlinks

Student Name:__________________________ **Date:**____________________

```
<HTML>
  <HEAD>
    <TITLE>Tipper Trucks R Us</TITLE>
  </HEAD>
  <BODY BGCOLOR=LIME>
    <P ALIGN=CENTER>
      <FONT SIZE=8 COLOR=MAROON FACE="lithograph">
        Tipper Trucks R Us
      </FONT>
    </P>
    <P ALIGN=CENTER>
      <IMG SRC="images/truck.jpg"
                WIDTH=150 HEIGHT=150>
    </P>
    <P ALIGN=CENTER>
      <FONT SIZE=3 COLOR=BLUE FACE="cooper black">
        Any size, Anytime, Anywhere!<BR>
        We have the truck you want!<BR>
        Call Us Now! on 01234 567890<BR>
      </FONT>
    </P>
    <P ALIGN=CENTER>
      <A HREF=”homepage.html”>
        Click here to enter
      </A>
    </P>
  </BODY>
</HTML>
```

Figure 4.1

Figure 4.2

1. Look at Figure 4.1 and write down the parameter and value that set the background colour.

   Parameter ____________________ Value _______________________

2. Which parameter of the `<FONT>` tag sets the colour of text, and which preset HTML colour is the dark red **Tipper Trucks R Us** title?

   Parameter ____________________ Preset Colour _________________

3. How should you spell the word **colour** in HTML code?

   a) COLORE ☐

   b) COLOR ☐

   c) COLOUR ☐

4. Write down all of the `<FONT>` tag information for the paragraph that starts **Any size, Anytime, Anywhere!**

   Size ___________ Colour ____________ Font Face ____________

5. Fill in the blanks in hexadecimal below:

Normal "Counting" Numbers	1	2	3	4	5	6	7	8	9	10	11	12	13	14	15	16
Hexadecimal Numbers	0	1					6	7		9		B	C			F

The colours of a rainbow are red, orange, yellow, green, blue, indigo and violet. But if you actually look at a rainbow, the colours fade smoothly from one to the next.
When you mix **primary** colours, red, yellow and blue (or red, green and blue on computers), you get what are called **secondary** colours. When you mix those, you create **tertiary** colours. So you can make *any* colour by mixing the primary colours in different ways.

Painters usually paint with tertiary colours because they are what you see in real life – you don't see the primary colours very often in nature. Tertiary colours are generally much nicer to look at. That is the reason why hexadecimal colours are so useful – the HTML preset colours only really let you use the very bright primary and secondary colours. With hexadecimal, you can make your backgrounds a little bit darker or lighter as you like.

This is the hexadecimal code for bright red:

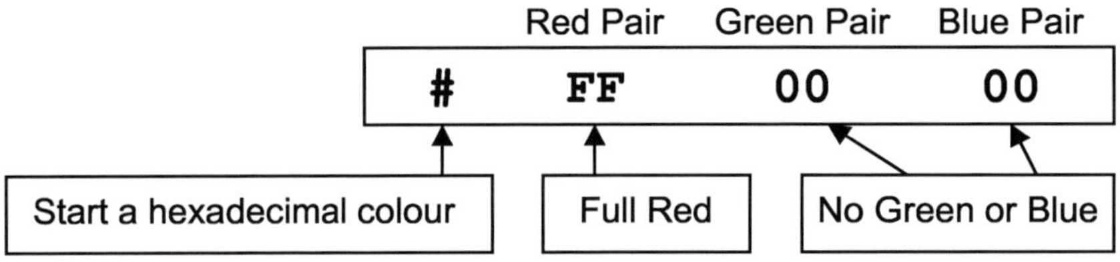

To make a slightly darker red, tone down the red pair from FF to 88, for example: `#880000`.
If you want a colour that is just the tiniest amount darker than that, try `#870000`. But that is such a small change, you probably won't be able to tell the difference!

6. Which of these is the code for bright blue?

   a) `#00FFFF` ☐

   b) `#FFFF00` ☐

   c) `#0000FF` ☐

7. Which of these is the code for bright green?

   a) `#0000FF` ☐

   b) `#00FF00` ☐

   c) `#000000` ☐

8. If you use something around 77 instead of the very strong FF, you get a gentler, darker shade of the computer primary colours, red, green and blue.

By mixing bright red and bright blue, you get pink. Purple is a mixture of the darker shades of red and blue. Which of these would give a purple colour?

a) #007777 ☐

b) #770077 ☐

c) #FF7700 ☐

9. Brown is a mixture of red, a bit less green and a small amount of blue. What is the code for brown?

a) #885522 ☐

b) #228855 ☐

c) #558822 ☐

10. Using light to paint with is a bit different from using paint on a brush. Black is made by having no colour at all and white is made by having all the colours at their strongest. Which of the hex codes below is white?

a) #007777 ☐

b) #000000 ☐

c) #FFFFFF ☐

d) #000077 ☐

11. White is a good colour for the background of an HTML page because it doesn't clash with any other colours.

It can make a web site look very smart, clear and professional. If you have some colour photos or pictures on a white background, a light grey border or menu would look very modern and stylish. Write the hex code for any light grey colour.

____

12. Visitors to a website need to get from one page to another. They do this by clicking on a hyperlink.

    Hyperlinks are written in this form:

```
<A HREF="name of the page you want to go to.html">
```

    The code in Figure 4.1 includes a hyperlink. Find it and write the name of the page that the hyperlink will take visitors to.

    ____

13. Imagine you clicked on the hyperlink in the browser in Figure 4.2 and it took you to another page. Which button in your browser would let you return to the **Tipper Trucks R Us** splash page?

    ____

14. If you put a hyperlink around an image, a thick blue border appears round the edge of the picture. Show how you would remove the border by filling in this incomplete `<IMG>` tag.

```
<A HREF="page2.html">
  <IMG SRC="button.gif" WIDTH=30 HEIGHT=15 ____________________ >
</A>
```

15. Usually, text hyperlinks are blue (and underlined). Fill in this `<BODY>` tag to show how you would change the colour of all the hyperlinks on a page to bright red.

```
<BODY BGCOLOR=#FFFFFF ______________________ >
```

16. Hyperlinks can be used to take a visitor to **any** web site on the Internet, not just another page in your own site. For example,

```
<A HREF="http://www.google.com">
```

    will take you to the Google search engine at **www.google.com**. The `http://` at the start just tells the browser how to find the site. If you forget to put it in, the link won't work!

    Look at this code. Complete the code for the links to **questions.html** (an imaginary page in your own web site) and **www.bbc.com/news**

```
<A HREF=" ______________________________ ">
  Click Here if you want to ask a question
</A>
<A HREF=" ______________________________ ">
  Click Here to catch up on the latest news
</A>
```

Basic HTML Teacher Resources
Worksheet 5A – Page Layout with Tables
Teacher's notes

Topics covered in this worksheet

- Table row tags, `<TR>`, and table data tags, `<TD>`
- Tables with images or other objects
- Nested tables
- Making a website 'map'

Tables can be a trying concept. It may be helpful to use colour-coded pieces of paper to help students get the feel of how the table tags enclose the table rows and the table rows enclose the table data. Drawing them out on paper is also useful.

Features which don't always do what is expected, such as use of `ROWSPAN` and `COLSPAN` parameters, can be understood by creating a new HTML document and just playing around with different combinations of rows, cells, alignment and the parameters `CELLSPACING`, `CELLPADDING`, `ROWSPAN`, `COLSPAN` and `BORDER`.

This comparison gives some of the optional extensions for the three table tag types:

<TABLE>		<TR>		<TD>	
Parameter	**Values**	**Parameter**	**Values**	**Parameter**	**Values**
`ALIGN` (sets the alignment of the table on the page)	`LEFT`, `RIGHT`, `CENTER`	`WIDTH` (sets minimum width of the row)	Any positive number	`ALIGN` (sets alignment of everything within a cell)	`LEFT`, `RIGHT`, `CENTER`
`BORDER` (sets the thickness of the border in and around the table)	Any positive number, or zero	`HEIGHT` (sets the minimum height of the row)	Any positive number	`ROWSPAN` (merge this cell with x cells below it)	Any positive number, x
`CELLPADDING` (keeps a distance between what is inside each cell and the cell border)	Any positive number, or zero			`COLSPAN` (merge this cell with x cells to the right)	Any positive number, x
`CELLSPACING` (distance between cells)	Any positive number, or zero			`BGCOLOR` (change the background colour of just this cell)	Preset or hex colour
`BACKGROUND` (use a picture or texture as the table background)	Any JPEG or GIF image in inverted commas, ie "car.jpg"			`WIDTH` (sets minimum width of the cell)	Any positive number
`BGCOLOR` (background colour of the whole table)	Preset or hex colour			`HEIGHT` (sets the minimum height of the cell)	Any positive number
`WIDTH` and `HEIGHT` (set min size for the table)	Any positive number				

Basic HTML
Worksheet 5A – Page Layout with Tables

Student Name:________________________ **Date:**___________________

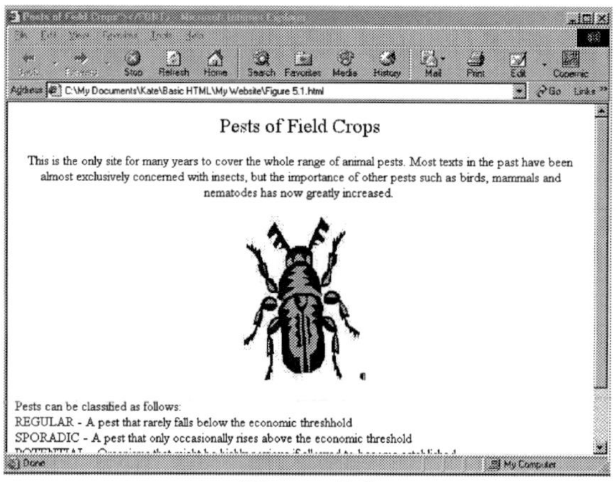

Figure 5.1

1. Look at Figure 5.1. It is a simple page where text and pictures follow each other down the page. How could you rearrange the page so that it looks much more interesting? Think about where you could put a menu so visitors can easily get to other parts of the site.

____

____

____

```
<TABLE ALIGN=LEFT WIDTH=250 HEIGHT=50 BGCOLOR=#AAAAFF BORDER=1>
  <TR>
    <TD>
      Cell 1
    </TD>
    <TD>
      Cell 2
    </TD>
  </TR>
  <TR>
    <TD>
      Cell 3
    </TD>
    <TD>
      Cell 4
    </TD>
  </TR>
</TABLE>
```

Figure 5.2

2. Look at the code for a table in Figure 5.2. How would you rewrite the `<TABLE>` tag to align the table to the middle of the page and to have no border?

____

3. The code in Figure 5.2 is for which table layout below?

a.

Cell 1
Cell 2
Cell 3
Cell 4

b.

Cell 1	Cell 3
Cell 2	Cell 4

c.

Cell 1	Cell 2
Cell 3	Cell 4

d.

	Cell 1	
Cell 2	Cell 3	
	Cell 4	

Answer __________

4. Describe the colour of the table background in Figure 5.2.

____

5. On Figure 5.2,
   Write the letter A next to the tag that starts the first row
   Write the letter B next to the tag that ends the first row
   Write the letter C next to the tag that starts the last cell
   Write the letter D next to the tag that ends the last cell

6. If you want to put pictures or writing into part of a table, where should they go? (Tick one box)

<TABLE> (your pictures or text) </TABLE> ☐

<TD> (your pictures or text) </TD> ☐

<TR> (your pictures or text) </TR> ☐

7. If you type an ALIGN parameter inside a <TD> tag, such as <TD ALIGN=RIGHT>, what will happen?

The cell will move closer to the right of the table ☐

Everything inside the cell will be aligned to the right. ☐

8. Nested tables give you even more control over the layout of your page. A nested table is just a table that's inside another table. Read Figure 5.3 and make sure you understand the way nesting tables allows you to design professional-looking web pages.

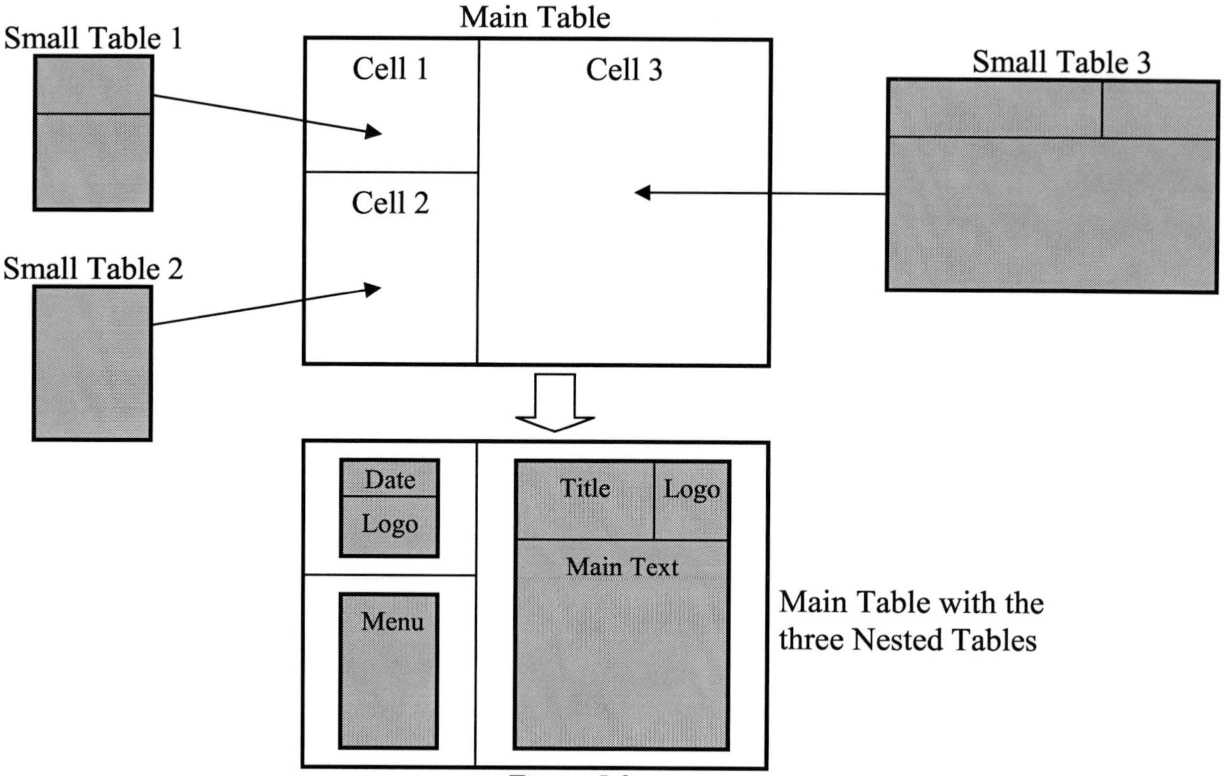

Figure 5.3

9. If you already have a table on your page, and you want to put a nested table inside it, where do you type the code for the nested table? (Tick one box)

<P> in here </P> ☐

<TR> in here </TR> ☐

<TD> or in here </TD> ☐

10. Look at the code in Figure 5.4 below. Draw a ring around the nested table.

```
<HTML><HEAD><TITLE>Fred's Site</TITLE></HEAD>
  <BODY>
    <TABLE WIDTH=400 HEIGHT=225 BORDER=1 BGCOLOR=#FFFF99>
      <TR>
        <TD>
          Welcome to Fred's Amazing Web Site
        </TD>
        <TD>
          <TABLE WIDTH=80 HEIGHT=60 BGCOLOR=WHITE CELLSPACING=1>
            <TR>
              <TD><B>Top TV Programs:</B></TD>
              <TD>1. Bill and Ben the Flower Pot men</TD>
              <TD>2. Thomas the Tank Engine</TD>
            </TR>
          </TABLE>
        </TD>
      </TR>
    </TABLE>
  </BODY>
</HTML>
```

Figure 5.4

11. Look at Figure 5.14 on Page 42 of *Basic HTML*. Why is it always a good idea to plan your web site before you begin coding?

____

____

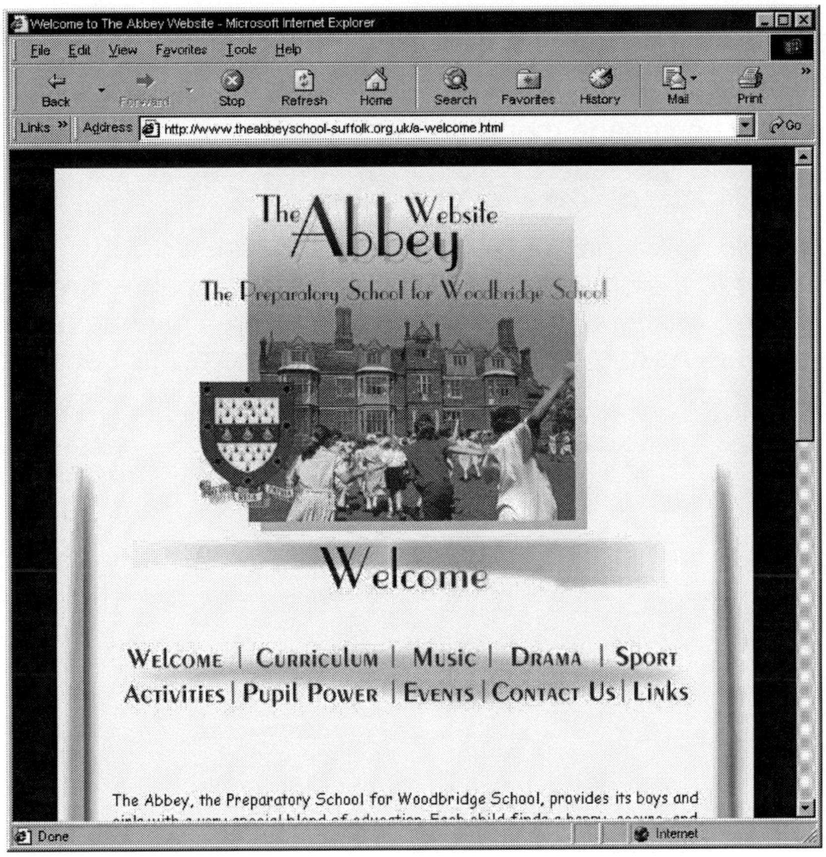

Figure 5.5

12. Figure 5.5 shows the home page (or, in this case, the *Welcome Page*) for a school web site. Suggest hexadecimal colours for the deep blue background and the light-yellow foreground.

Background ____________________ Foreground ____________________

13. Fill in the site plan below for the web site in Figure 5.5.

Splash Page

↓

Welcome Page (in Figure 5.5)

Basic HTML Teacher Resources
Worksheet 6A – Building Your Homepage
Teacher's notes

Topics covered in this worksheet

- The homepage as the centre of a web site
- Hyperlinks to other pages
- Use of tables in a homepage menu
- File extensions

A homepage should make the subject matter of the website very plain and show clear, intuitive links to the other pages. Planning a homepage carefully will save hours of frustration to visitors. If it is really bad they may give up and not bother to enter the site proper. Asking for examples of good and awful websites often gives rise to fruitful comment.

Basic HTML
Worksheet 6A – Building your Home Page

Student Name:________________________ **Date:________________**

The home page is the centre of your website. It has to look good and show visitors how to navigate your web site. Read Figure 6.2 and see how it forms Figure 6.1.

Figure 6.1

```
<HTML>
  <HEAD><TITLE>Cool Cats Home Page</TITLE></HEAD>
  <BODY BGCOLOR=WHITE TEXT=GRAY LINK=GRAY VLINK="#606060">
    <IMG SRC="images/white.gif" WIDTH=1 HEIGHT=40>
<!-- menu table -->
    <TABLE ALIGN=CENTER CELLSPACING=0 CELLPADDING=0>
      <TR><TD COLSPAN=6><IMG SRC="images/grey.gif" WIDTH=500 HEIGHT=1></TD></TR>
      <TR HEIGHT=30>
        <TD ALIGN=CENTER><IMG SRC="images/arrow.gif"><A HREF="homepage.html">Home Page</A></TD>
        <TD ALIGN=CENTER><IMG SRC="images/arrow.gif"><A HREF="kittens.html">Kittens</A></TD>
        <TD ALIGN=CENTER><IMG SRC="images/arrow.gif"><A HREF="older.html">Older Cats</A></TD>
        <TD ALIGN=CENTER><IMG SRC="images/arrow.gif"><A HREF="best.html">Best Breeds</A></TD>
        <TD ALIGN=CENTER><IMG SRC="images/arrow.gif"><A HREF="catfood.html">Cat Food</A></TD>
        <TD ALIGN=CENTER><IMG SRC="images/arrow.gif"><A HREF="faq.html">Cats FAQ</A></TD>
      </TR>
      <TR><TD COLSPAN=6><IMG SRC="images/grey.gif" WIDTH=500 HEIGHT=1></TD></TR>
    </TABLE>
<!-- table with heading and picture -->
    <TABLE WIDTH=450 ALIGN=CENTER CELLSPACING=0 CELLPADDING=0>
      <TR>
        <TD WIDTH=175 ALIGN=CENTER>
          <FONT SIZE=5 COLOR=BLUE>Cool Cats<BR>Home Page</FONT><BR>
          <FONT SIZE=2 FACE="arial">
            <P>Welcome to my web site all about cats!<BR>
               Please use the links above to look around.</P>
          </FONT>
        </TD>
        <TD><IMG SRC="images/cornflake.jpg" WIDTH=300 HEIGHT=195></TD>
      </TR>
    </TABLE>
<!-- copyright table -->
    <TABLE ALIGN=CENTER CELLSPACING=0 CELLPADDING=0>
      <TR><TD><IMG SRC="images/grey.gif" WIDTH=500 HEIGHT=1></TD></TR>
      <TR HEIGHT=30>
        <TD ALIGN=RIGHT><FONT SIZE=2 FACE="arial">Copyright C. R. Hayhow, 2002</FONT></TD>
      </TR>
      <TR><TD><IMG SRC="images/grey.gif" WIDTH=500 HEIGHT=1></TD></TR>
    </TABLE>

  </BODY>
</HTML>
```

Figure 6.2

1. On the lines below, write a list of all the links shown in Figure 6.1. On the other lines below to the right, write the names of web pages that the links go to (by finding the right code in Figure 6.2).

____________________	____________________
____________________	____________________
____________________	____________________
____________________	____________________
____________________	____________________
____________________	____________________

2. In Figure 6.2, find the code that puts the first horizontal grey line across the web page. Write down the image file it uses and how wide it is.

   Image File ____________________ Width ____________________

3. a) How many tables are there in Figure 6.2? ____________________

   b) Are there any nested tables? ____________________

4. Write down the three HTML comment tags used in Figure 6.2.

   ____

   ____

   ____

5. Comment tags can help you keep track of where you are in the HTML code for a page. This is especially useful for long HTML pages where there is lots of code.

   Do you see comments when you view a page in a browser? __________

6. Graphics for web pages are usually in JPEG graphics format (.jpg files).

   What is the other main image format that can be used in web pages?

   ____

7. The little arrows to the left of each menu item in Figure 6.1 are actually animations.

   a) Which image format must the arrow be in? ____________________

   b) What is the name of the arrow image? ____________________

   c) Which folder is it in? ____________________

8. Compare Figures 6.1 and 6.2 again. The first table is at the top of the page. It has three rows. The first row and the third row just have a horizontal grey line. In between them, the second row has the six links and images.

   a) How many cells are there in the second row? ________________

   b) How many cells are there in the first row or the third row? ________

   c) What would happen if there was no `COLSPAN=6` parameter in the first or the third rows?

   ____

   ____

   ____

9. There is a blank space in the browser window in Figure 6.3. Design a different home page for the "Cool Cats" web site in the space. Try to think about how you would write the code to make your new design while you are drawing it.

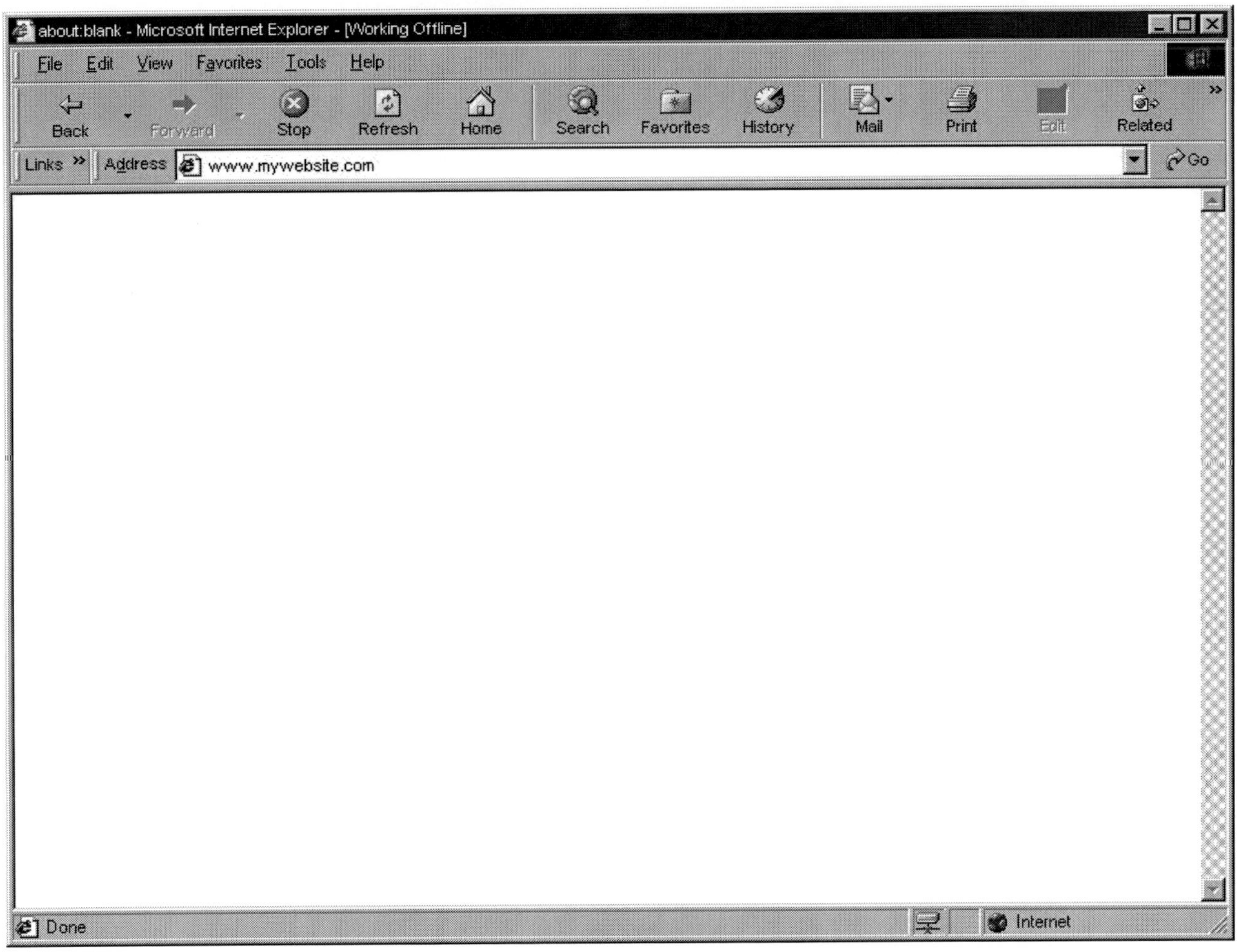

Figure 6.3

Basic HTML Teacher Resources
Worksheet 7A – Multimedia
Teacher's notes

Topics covered in this worksheet

- Multimedia items that can be used on a website
- Sound file properties
- Inserting sound and video clips
- Applet tags

Students can really have fun with multimedia on their web pages. It is prudent to point out that 'small is beautiful' and too much happening on a page can be both confusing and off-putting.

Students should also be aware that some files may be very large, video clips particularly, and thought should be given to how long it takes to open a page. Visitors will get frustrated if the game or clip they want to see takes too long to download. Examples from the class will bring this point home.

Basic HTML
Worksheet 7A – Multimedia

Student Name:______________________ **Date:________________**

Multimedia can make your web site really exciting and stamp it with your own personality.

1. Which of the following items could be displayed as part of a multimedia web site?

   a) Video clips ☐

   b) Microsoft Word document ☐

   c) Sound files ☐

   d) Java Applets ☐

2. Give an example of an audio format that gives high quality sound?

   ____

3. What is a disadvantage of using the WAV audio format?

   ____

   ____

```
<EMBED SRC="sounds/hello.wav" AUTOSTART=TRUE LOOP=FALSE
                        ALIGN=CENTER WIDTH=1 HEIGHT=1>
</EMBED>
```

Figure 7.1 A sound file

4. Look at Figure 7.1. The value of the `SRC` parameter shows the browser which file to load. What does SRC stand for?

   ____

```
...
  <EMBED SRC="videos/tiger-prowling.mpg" ALIGN=RIGHT
        AUTOSTART=TRUE WIDTH=320 HEIGHT=192 LOOP=FALSE>
  </EMBED>
...
```

Figure 7.2 A video clip

5. Figure 7.2 is an extract of HTML code that will embed a video clip in a web page. What is the file name of the video clip file, and which folder is it in?

   File ______________________ Folder ________________

6. Where would the clip in Figure 7.2 appear on the web page, and what size would it be?

   Alignment ____________ Width _______ Height _______ Units ________

```
<APPLET CODE="javagame.class" WIDTH=300 HEIGHT=250>
  <PARAM NAME="bullets" VALUE="20">
  <PARAM NAME="speed" VALUE="200">

<_______________>
```

Some Java Applets have these extra <PARAM> tags to allow you to change some of their properties.

Figure 7.3

7. Why is it best not to put too many flashy, moving items on a web page?

   ____

   ____

8. Games and other features can be added to a website by using Java Applets. Figure 7.3 shows some code for doing this. The Applet is **javagame.class**. Fill in the blank line in Figure 7.3 that would close the Applet tag.

9. The Applet in Figure 7.3 has no `ALIGN` parameter at the moment. Give **three** ways you could align the Applet to the centre of the page.
   Hint: Try to think which kind of tags can have the `ALIGN` parameter.

____

____

____

____

____

____

Basic HTML Teacher Resources
Worksheet 8A – Uploading by FTP
Teacher's notes

Topics covered in this worksheet

- Function of FTP
- ISPs
- Usernames and passwords

File Transfer Protocol (FTP) software allows you to transfer files to a server. There are thousands and thousands of servers around the world, each having a different purpose. Many of them allow people to 'upload' their web sites so they can be visited by members of the public. This is called web hosting.

Some web hosts allow you to upload your web site for free; some will place an advert banner on your site; some may charge a initialisation fee and some may ask you to pay for the service.

For class purposes, use a free server. Although the connection may not always be as fast or reliable as commercial hosts, they provide a valuable way to set up a first web site. At this level, there is really no difference between a free server and the most expensive server-only businesses requiring database access or server-side tools will benefit.

A list of good, free internet service providers (ISPs) offering simple, free hosting can be found at www.payne-gallway.co.uk/basichtml/worksheets.

Basic HTML
Worksheet 8A – Uploading by FTP

Student Name:_______________________ **Date:**__________________

1. What does FTP stand for?

   F _ _ _ T _ _ _ _ _ _ _ _ P _ _ _ _ _ _ _ _

2. What can you use FTP to do?

   ____

3. Once you have uploaded your web site to the Internet, you can still edit it on your own computer. To change the copy of your web site that is on the Internet, just connect using FTP and replace the old file with the new one from your computer. How does the FTP service make sure that nobody else can change your web site, once you have uploaded it?

   ____

4. What does ISP stand for?

   I _ _ _ _ _ _ _ _ _ S _ _ _ _ _ _ _ _ P _ _ _ _ _ _ _ _ _

5. Some ISPs allow you to upload your web site on their server so that the whole world can view it. Suppose you want to put a web site onto the Internet; in which order should you do these things?

   a) Upload your web site to the Internet, using FTP.

   b) Check your web site for mistakes.

   c) Find a good ISP and register with them to get a username, password and a place to put your web site (your web address).

   d) Write your web site.

   e) Check your web address to see your web site in action!

   Put the letters in the correct order here ____________________________

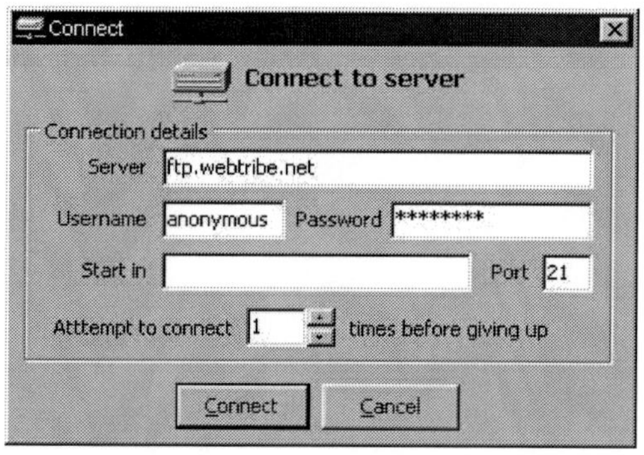

Figure 8.1

6. Look at Figure 8.1. It shows a simple FTP program which is about to connect to a web server. Which server will the web site be saved to?

____

7. People often miss little mistakes in their code. It is important to check through completely before uploading a web page because some browsers show the wrong thing when they come across a mistake.

   There are 3 errors in Figure 8.2. Put a ring around the line number on the left where there is a mistake, and then write out the line correctly below.

```
1  <HTML>
2    <HEAD>
3      <TITLE>Famous Detectives<TITLE>
4    </HEAD>
5    <BODY>
6      <P ALIGN=CENTER>
7        <IMG SRC="images/sherlock.jpj" WIDTH=200 HEIGHT=300>
8      </P>
9      <P ALIGN=LEFT>
10       <FONT SIZE=4 FACE="times new roman"" COLOR=#562398>
11         Join the Great Detectives and solve some of the<BR>
12         World's Greatest Mysteries!>
13       </FONT>
14     </P>
15   </BODY>
16 </HTML>
```

Figure 8.2

____

____

____

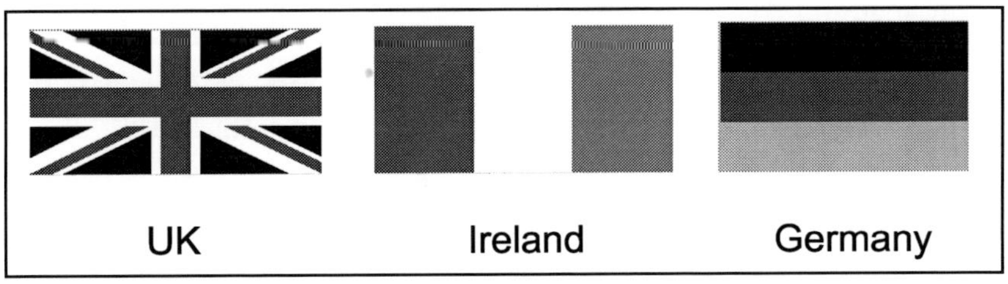

Figure 8.3

8. Lastly, because hexadecimal colours can be tricky, look at Figure 8.3. It shows the UK, Irish and German flags. Write down which flag has the colours of the code below.

```
#72AA15     #FFFFFF     #EE6600
```

Flag ________________

HTML Information Sheet for Pupils

An HTML tag is a command inside angled brackets, like this: <P>
Tags can be extended so that their behaviour is slightly different: <P ALIGN=RIGHT>

Parameter   Value

Some of the tags that allow you to create a table can be quite difficult to understand. Use this guide to help you understand how to write HTML tables if you get stuck:

<TABLE>		<TR>		<TD>	
Parameter	**Values**	**Parameter**	**Values**	**Parameter**	**Values**
ALIGN (sets the alignment of the table on the page)	LEFT, RIGHT, CENTER	WIDTH (sets minimum width of the row)	Any positive number	ALIGN (sets alignment of everything within a cell)	LEFT, RIGHT, CENTER
BORDER (sets the thickness of the border in and around the table)	Any positive number, or zero	HEIGHT (sets the minimum height of the row)	Any positive number	ROWSPAN (merge this cell with x cells below it)	Any positive number, x
CELLPADDING (keeps a distance between what is inside each cell and the cell border)	Any positive number, or zero			COLSPAN (merge this cell with x cells to the right)	Any positive number, x
CELLSPACING (distance between cells)	Any positive number, or zero			BGCOLOR (change the background colour of just this cell)	Preset or hex colour
BACKGROUND (use a picture or texture as the table background)	Any JPEG or GIF image in inverted commas, ie "car.jpg"			WIDTH (sets minimum width of the cell)	Any positive number
BGCOLOR (background colour of the whole table)	Preset or hex colour			HEIGHT (sets the minimum height of the cell)	Any positive number
WIDTH and HEIGHT (set min size for the table)	Any positive number				

Answers

1A – HTML and the Internet

1. HyperText Markup Language
   HTML is a simple 'scripting' language. A browser program reads the script and displays a page on the screen.
2. As an individual's homepage (e.g. about a hobby); as a source of information (e.g. Weather Forecast); as a company's web site (e.g. to buy CDs or books); as a place to download programs, sound files, graphics and so on (e.g. clipart); to advertise something (e.g. a list of good toy shops).
3. a. browser b. editor
4. b. (An editor)
5. Any two web sites with information about how they are used.
6. d. (Anyone in the world)
7. Open the folder **C:** from **My Computer**, select **New Folder** from the **File** menu. The name of the new folder can then be entered.
8. a. Start Menu b. Taskbar
9. It can vary, but usually by opening **Programs** from the **Start Menu** and selecting **Internet Explorer**. (When using the Windows Operating System)
10. Tick all apart from c.
    All web pages are displayed using HTML. If a special software package can add a feature to a web page, then typing the correct code into an editor will have the same effect.
    The main advantage of special web design programs is the way they help organise your web site. They also allow web pages to be developed by drawing tables, resizing graphics and so on. Such programs are called WYSIWYG (What You See Is What You Get)
11. Multimedia, good layout, attractive graphics and designs, useful headings, good use of colour.

2A – Writing HTML

1. a. <HTML>
   b. </HTML>
2. </P> will end a paragraph.
3. The parameter is ALIGN, the value is LEFT.
4.

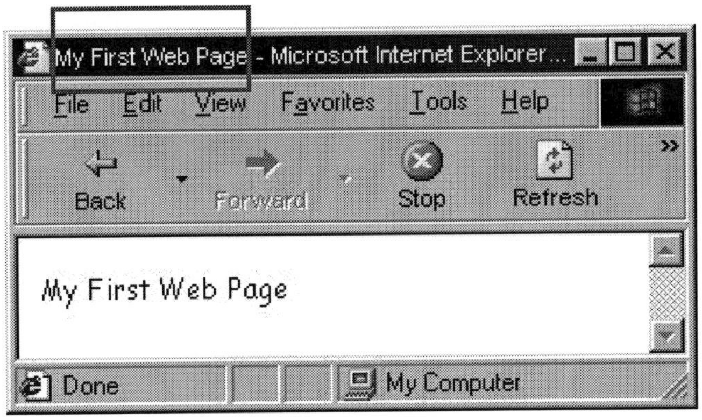

5. Refresh or Reload. (depends on the browser)
6. CENTER
7.

8.

```
<P ALIGN=CENTER>
  Drop dead gorgeous nuggets of Finest Flour,<BR>
  Fried to a Golden Brown and Dusted with Demerara Sugar<BR>
  then rolled in Technicolor Hundreds and Thousands.<BR>
  Your mouth will love you forever!
</P>
```

9. 1) **Write** the HTML code in an editor.
   2) **Save** the code as an HTML file. (Note: Don't forget to select **All Files (*.*)** the first time you save!)
   3) View the page in a **browser.**

3A – Graphics and Fonts

1. <IMG>
2. Size parameters for the <IMG> tag are WIDTH and HEIGHT.
3. Pixel(s) (Stands for *Picture Element(s)*, the tiny dots that make up a bitmap image)
4. <IMG SRC="my-picture.jpg" WIDTH=80 HEIGHT=100> (The parameters can be put in any order in HTML tags, so WIDTH could go after HEIGHT and so on)
5. c. (Portraits are taller than they are wide, whereas landscape paintings are wide but not very tall. These terms are now also used to describe the format of items on a page, or the page layout itself.)
6. In Figure 3.2, the smallest is size used is size 2, and the largest is size 7.
7. The smallest size allowed in HTML is 1, and the largest is size 7. (However, larger numbers may work in some browsers.) The HTML font size is not related to font sizes in word processors.
8. a. <U> and </U>
   b. <B> and </B> (also <STRONG> and </STRONG>)
   c. <I> and </I>
9. The FACE parameter.
10. <B><FONT SIZE=4 FACE="comic sans ms">hello</FONT></B>
    or <FONT SIZE=4 FACE="comic sans ms"><B>hello</B></FONT>

4A – Colours and Hyperlinks

1. Parameter is BGCOLOR, value is LIME.
2. Parameter is COLOR, preset colour used is MAROON.
3. b. (COLOR)
4. Size is 3, colour is BLUE, and font face is "cooper black".
5.

1	2	3	4	5	6	7	8	9	10	11	12	13	14	15	16
0	1	**2**	**3**	**4**	**5**	6	7	**8**	9	**A**	B	C	**D**	**E**	F

6. c. #0000FF
7. b. #00FF00
8. b. #770077
9. a. #885522
10. c. #FFFFFF
11. #A0A0A0 or #AAAAAA or #C3C3C3 and so on. (So long as the red pair, green pair and blue pair are identical, a grey colour will result.)
12. "homepage.html"
13. The **Back** button (usually a left arrow on the toolbar of the browser program).
14. BORDER=0 (in the space provided)
15. LINK=#FF0000 (in the space provided)

16.

```
<A HREF="questions.html">
  Click Here if you want to ask a question
</A>
<A HREF="http://www.bbc.com/news">
  Click Here to catch up on the latest news
</A>
```

5A – Page Layout with Tables

1. Use a table to make the layout more interesting, and place a navigation menu in a convenient place such as the left-hand side or the top of the page.
2. `<TABLE ALIGN=CENTER WIDTH=250 HEIGHT=50 BGCOLOR=#FFFFCC BORDER=0>`
3. c.
4. Light blue (full blue pair, and fairly high red and green pairs to brighten the colour)
5. (Figure 5.2)

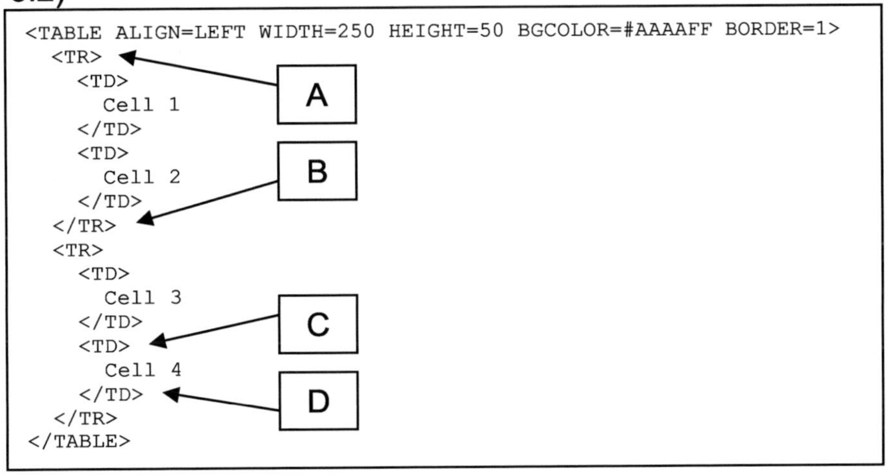

6. b. (between <TD> and </TD>)
7. b. Everything inside the cell will be aligned to the right. (Or rather the *default* alignment for everything within the cell will be to the right – individual objects/text can be aligned differently by putting them inside paragraph tags)
8. (No answer)
9. c. (Because no matter what is to be put into a table, whether it's a normal HTML object or a nested table, it must go between the <TD> and </TD> tags)

10. (Figure 5.4)

```
<HTML><HEAD><TITLE>Fred's Site</TITLE></HEAD>
  <BODY>
    <TABLE WIDTH=400 HEIGHT=225 BORDER=1 BGCOLOR=#FFFF99>
      <TR>
        <TD>
          Welcome to Fred's Amazing Web Site
        </TD>
        <TD>
          <TABLE WIDTH=80 HEIGHT=60 BGCOLOR=WHITE CELLSPACING=1>
            <TR>
              <TD><B>Top TV Programs:</B></TD>
              <TD>1. Bill and Ben the Flower Pot men</TD>
              <TD>2. Thomas the Tank Engine</TD>
            </TR>
          </TABLE>
        </TD>
      </TR>
    </TABLE>
  </BODY>
</HTML>
```

Nested Table

11. To help foresee any problems; to decide how many pages to create; gain an impression of the layout of the site; it's best not to jump straight in and begin coding, but rather to stand back and decide how and what to do.
12. Background is #3333AA (or similar - dark blue, i.e. the last colour pair is a mid-range value, and the other pairs have much smaller values)
    Foreground is #FFFADE (or similar - e.g. full red and nearly full green, plus a bit of the remaining colour, in this case blue, to lighten it. In computer primary colours, the RGB system, yellow is made by mixing red and green)
13. Nine other pages stemming from the Welcome Page box: Curriculum, Music, Drama, Sport, Activities, Pupil Power, Events, Contact Us, Links. (In any order)

6A – Building your Home Page

1. | | |
   |---|---|
   | Home Page | homepage.html |
   | Kittens | kittens.html |
   | Older Cats | older.html |
   | Best Breeds | best.html |
   | Cat Food | catfood.html |
   | Cats FAQ | faq.html |
2. File is either images/grey.gif or just grey.gif (preferred), and width is 500 pixels.
3. a. 3
   b. No. (There are no nested tables)
4. <!-- menu table -->
   <!-- table with heading and picture -->
   <!-- copyright table -->
5. No. (Comments are only visible in the editor)
6. GIF images (.gif files)
7. a. It must be in the **GIF** format to be an animation.
   b. arrow.gif
   c. images
8. a. 6 cell in the second row
   b. 1 cell in the first row (same as third row)

c. The grey line would only be as wide as the first button. By adding COLSPAN=6, the cell with the grey line can span across all of the buttons.

9. Any sensible design.

7A – Multimedia

1. a. c. d. (Not b.)
2. WAV audio format.
3. WAV files are very large, even for short bursts of sound, so they take a long time to load.
4. SRC stands for Source (the source of an image file could be <IMG SRC="xxx/yyy/zzz/picture.jpg"> for example)
5. File is tiger-prowling.mpg, folder is videos.
6. Alignment is RIGHT, width is 320, height is 192, units are pixels.
7. Animations and other multimedia elements take much longer to load than normal HTML text and pictures; they make the computer work harder to display and play them all; they can distract attention from the information on a page; they may not work in all browsers.
8. /APPLET in the blank space so the last line of Figure 7.3 becomes </APPLET>
9. In any order:
   1. Set the ALIGN parameter of the <APPLET> tag to have the value CENTER.
   2. Put the Applet in a paragraph (between <P ALIGN=CENTER> and </P>) tags.
   3. Put the Applet in a table, and align the table to the centre of the page: <TABLE ALIGN=CENTER><TR><TD>Applet in here</TD></TR></TABLE>

8A – Uploading by FTP

1. <u>File</u> <u>Transfer</u> <u>Protocol</u>
2. FTP is used to upload a web site, or parts of a web site, to a server (which will allow other people to view your site). It can also be used to download files, but that is not such an important feature here.
3. FTP has a password protection mechanism, so only people who know the correct username and password can change your web site. Keep passwords safe!
4. <u>Internet</u> <u>Service</u> <u>Provider</u>
5. Correct order: d. b. c. a. e.
6. ftp.webtribe.net, although the server name is actually webtribe.net. The "ftp." at the start will be recognised and converted to "ftp://ftp.webtribe.net" to tell the server that we want to connect using the FTP service. Similarly, when you view a page in a browser you type www.webtribe.net, which is converted to "http://www.webtribe.net" because, to view the page, the browser uses the HTTP service. HTTP, which is how all web pages are viewed, is faster that FTP but includes no way to upload (to save) files. HTTP is read only. For this reason, both FTP and HTTP services are required to be running on any web server.
7. Mistakes:
   Line 3: <TITLE>Famous Detectives</TITLE>
   Line 7: <IMG SRC="images/sherlock.jp**g**" WIDTH=200 HEIGHT=300>
   Line 12: World's Greatest Mysteries! (Should be no '**>**' after 'Mysteries!')
8. Flag is Irish. (Green, White, Orange)

Basic HTML
Answer Sheet 1A – HTML and the Internet

Student Name:____________________ **Date:**________________

1. ______________________________

2. a) ______________________________

   b) ______________________________

   c) ______________________________

   d) ______________________________

3. a) ______________ b) ______________

4. a) ☐ b) ☐ c) ☐

5. a) ______________________________

   ____

   b) ______________________________

   ____

6. a) ☐ b) ☐ c) ☐ d) ☐

7. ______________________________

   ____

   ____

8. a) ______________ b) ______________

9. ______________________________

   ____

10. a. b. c. d.

11. ______________________________

Basic HTML
Answer Sheet 2A – Writing HTML

Student Name:________________________ **Date:**__________________

1. a) ______________________ b) ______________________

2. ____

3. Parameter __________________ Value ______________________

4.

5. ____

6. a) ☐ b) ☐ c) ☐

7. __________

8.

```
<P ALIGN=CENTER>
  Drop dead gorgeous nuggets of Finest Flour,
  Fried to a Golden Brown and Dusted with Demerara Sugar
  then rolled in Technicolor Hundreds and Thousands.
  Your mouth will love you forever!
</P>
```

9. a) W _ _ _ _ the HTML code in an editor

   b) S _ _ _ the code as an HTML file

   c) View the page in a b _ _ _ _ _ _

Basic HTML
Answer Sheet 3A – Graphics and Fonts

Student Name:_______________________ **Date:__________________**

1. ___________________________

2. ___________________________ ___________________________

3. ___________________________

4. ____

5. a) ☐ b) ☐ c) ☐

6. Smallest ____________________ Largest ____________________

7. Smallest ____________________ Largest ____________________

8. a) Underlined _______ _______

   b) Bold _______ _______

   c) Italic _______ _______

9. ___________________

10. ____

Basic HTML
Answer Sheet 4A – Colours and Hyperlinks

Student Name:________________________ **Date:**__________________

1. Parameter ____________________ Value _______________________

2. Parameter ____________________ Preset Colour ________________

3. a) ☐ b) ☐ c) ☐

4. Size __________ Colour__________ Font Face __________

5.

Normal "Counting" Numbers	1	2	3	4	5	6	7	8	9	10	11	12	13	14	15	16
Hexadecimal Numbers	0	1					6	7		9		B	C			F

6. a) ☐ b) ☐ c) ☐

7. a) ☐ b) ☐ c) ☐

8. a) ☐ b) ☐ c) ☐

9. a) ☐ b) ☐ c) ☐

10. a) ☐ b) ☐ c) ☐ d) ☐

11. # _________________________

12. ____

13. ____

14.

```
<A HREF="page2.html">
  <IMG SRC="button.gif" WIDTH=30 HEIGHT=15 ____________________ >
</A>
```

15.

```
<BODY BGCOLOR=#FFFFFF ______________________ >
```

16.

```
<A HREF=" ______________________________ ">
  Click Here if you want to ask a question
</A>
<A HREF=" ______________________________ ">
  Click Here to catch up on the latest news
</A>
```

Basic HTML
Answer Sheet 5A – Page Layout with Tables

Student Name:________________________ **Date:**__________________

1. ____

____

____

2. ____

3. Answer _________

4. ____

5.

```
<TABLE ALIGN=LEFT WIDTH=250 HEIGHT=50 BGCOLOR=#AAAAFF BORDER=1>
  <TR>
    <TD>
      Cell 1
    </TD>
    <TD>
      Cell 2
    </TD>
  </TR>
  <TR>
    <TD>
      Cell 3
    </TD>
    <TD>
      Cell 4
    </TD>
  </TR>
</TABLE>
```

6. a) ☐ b) ☐ c) ☐

7. a) ☐ b) ☐

9. a) ☐ b) ☐ c) ☐

10.

```
<HTML><HEAD><TITLE>Fred's Site</TITLE></HEAD>
  <BODY>
    <TABLE WIDTH=400 HEIGHT=225 BORDER=1 BGCOLOR=#FFFF99>
      <TR>
        <TD>
          Welcome to Fred's Amazing Web Site
        </TD>
        <TD>
          <TABLE WIDTH=80 HEIGHT=60 BGCOLOR=WHITE CELLSPACING=1>
            <TR>
              <TD><B>Top TV Programs:</B></TD>
              <TD>1. Bill and Ben the Flower Pot men</TD>
              <TD>2. Thomas the Tank Engine</TD>
            </TR>
          </TABLE>
        </TD>
      </TR>
    </TABLE>
  </BODY>
</HTML>
```

11. ____

____

12. Background ____________________ Foreground ____________________

13.

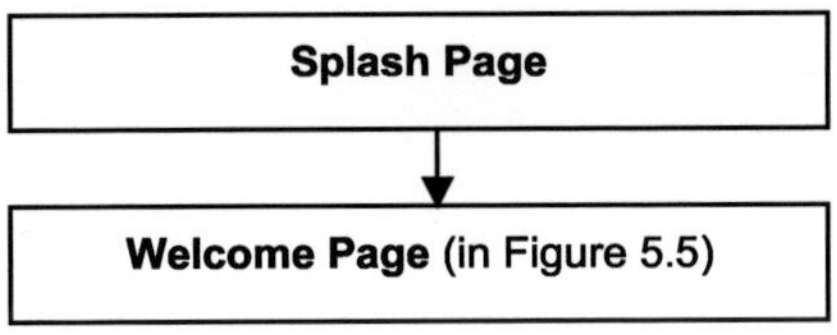

Basic HTML
Answer Sheet 6A – Building your Home Page

Student Name:________________________ **Date:____________________**

1. ____________________ ____________________

2. Image File ____________ Width ____________

3. a) ________________

   b) ________________

4. ________________________________

5. ________________

6. ________________________________

7. a) ________________

   b) ________________

   c) ________________

8. a) ________________

   b) ________________

   c) ________________________________

Basic HTML
Answer Sheet 7A – Multimedia

Student Name:________________________ **Date:**__________________

1. a) ☐ b) ☐ c) ☐ d) ☐

2. ____

3. ____

____

4. ____

5. File __________________________ Folder ____________________

6. Alignment ____________ Width _______ Height _______ Units ________

7. ____

____

8.

```
<APPLET CODE="javagame.class" WIDTH=300 HEIGHT=250>
  <PARAM NAME="bullets" VALUE="20">
  <PARAM NAME="speed" VALUE="200">

<______________>
```

9. ____

____

____

____

____

____

Basic HTML
Answer Sheet 8A – Uploading by FTP

Student Name:________________________ **Date:**__________________

1. F _ _ _   T _ _ _ _ _ _ _ _   P _ _ _ _ _ _ _ _
2. ____
3. ____
4. I _ _ _ _ _ _ _ _   S _ _ _ _ _ _ _   P _ _ _ _ _ _ _ _
5. Correct Order ____
6. ____
7. ____

   ____

   ____
8. Flag ________________

Basic HTML

Teacher Resources

Series B

PAYNE-GALLWAY
PUBLISHERS LTD

Basic HTML Teacher Resources
Worksheet 1B – HTML and the Internet
Teacher's notes

Topics covered in this worksheet

- Using View Source to look at code on a web page
- Making folders for a charity web site
- Downloading files from the Internet

This worksheet is intended to introduce students to looking critically at html code on the Internet. They will ultimately get some good ideas from it! Professional code does not always follow best practice in using capital letters and including all end tags, so emphasise the importance of obeying the rules when they are learning.

Individual computers and networks may not use exactly the same paths to programs as those shown in this worksheet. It would be prudent to check which methods best suit your platform.

It may help to add a Shortcut to Notepad on the desktop (or each pupil's work directory) so that the tedious trawl through the start menu to find Notepad can be avoided.
This can be done by right-clicking on the background of the desktop (or the background of the chosen directory) and selecting **Shortcut** from the **New** menu that appears on the pop-up selection. Type **C:\Windows\Notepad.exe** where it says "Command Line:" (or find **Notepad.exe** using the "browse" button) and press **Next**. Type **Notepad** in the "name" box and press **Finish**. You will see a new icon on the screen. Double-click on it to launch Notepad.

Alternatively, select **Run…** from the **Start** menu. To open Notepad, type **notepad** and press Enter. To open the Internet Explorer browser, type **iexplore** instead. To run Microsoft Paint, type **mspaint**, and so on. The Run… command remembers what you typed last time, so it can be a very fast tool to use.

Once a basic understanding of the HTML syntax has been achieved, it may benefit faster students if they go to their favourite web sites and view the source code (by right-clicking on the background of the browser window and selecting **View**, **Source**). An insight into professional web design may give them more ideas about how to create their own site.

Basic HTML
Worksheet 1B – HTML and the Internet

Student Name:________________________ **Date:**___________________

In this worksheet you will log on to the Internet and look at some web pages. You will then have a look at how web pages work by viewing their "source code". Finally you will prepare your computer so that you can create a Charity Web Site throughout the rest of these worksheets.

1. Log on to the Internet and in a browser program, open the page **www.payne-gallway.co.uk/basichtml/worksheets**

2. Click on the link **Specimen Web Pages**.

3. Find the link to **tippertrucks.html** and click on it to view the "Tipper Trucks R Us" page.

4. Right-click on the green background of the web page and select **View Source** from the pop-up menu.

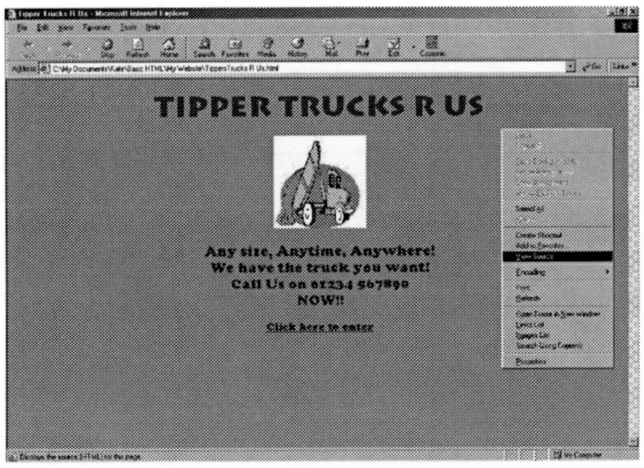

Figure 1.1

5. A new window should appear on the screen showing the special HTML instructions, called **code**, that make the page look the way it does.

```
<HTML><HEAD><TITLE>Tipper Trucks R Us</TITLE></HEAD>

  <BODY BGCOLOR=LIME>

    <P ALIGN=CENTER>
      <FONT SIZE=7 FONT COLOR=MAROON FONT FACE="lithograph">Tipper Trucks R Us</FONT>
    </P>
     <P ALIGN=CENTER>
       <IMG SRC="images/tipper truck.jpg" WIDTH=150 HEIGHT=150>
     </P>
     <P ALIGN=CENTER>
       <FONT SIZE=5 FONT COLOR=BLUE FONT FACE="cooper black">Any size, Anytime,
Anywhere!<BR>We have the truck you want!<BR>Call Us on 01234
567890<BR>NOW!!</FONT></FONT>
     </P>
     <P ALIGN=CENTER>
       <A HREF="homepage.html">
        <FONT SIZE=4 FONT COLOR=BLUE FONT FACE="cooper black">Click here to enter</FONT>
       </A>
```

Figure 1.2

6. Look through the code. You will see many angular brackets containing various commands, such as `<HTML>` and `</P>`. These are called **tags**, and are used to describe how the web page appears in a browser.

7. When you have had a good look through the code, close the new window. You should now see your browser program again. Click on the **Back** button in your browser and open the page called **cats.html**.

8. View the source code for the "Cool Cats" page by selecting **Source** from the **View** menu in the browser, or by right-clicking on the white background of the page and selecting **View Source**.

9. Try to find some similarities between this code and the code for the "Tipper Trucks" page. In Chapter 2 of *Basic HTML*, and in the next worksheet, you will learn how to create your own code. It's not as difficult as it looks!

10. Close the code window and your browser, then disconnect from the Internet.

Now you are going to make the folders in which to put all your Charity Web Site files.

11. From the **Start** menu select **Programs**, **Windows Explorer**.

12. Double click on the first hard disk (**C:**) icon.

13. Select **New**, **Folder** from the **File** menu. Name the folder **HTMLworksheet** and press Enter.

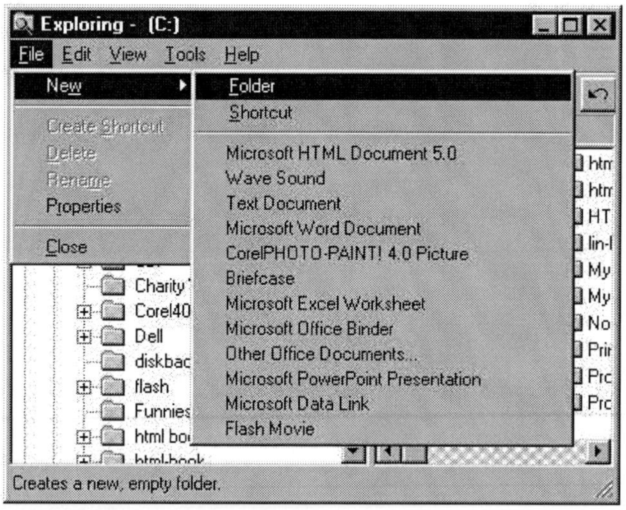

Figure 1.3

14. Open your new **HTMLworksheet** folder by double-clicking on it. Now create three new folders there, called **Images**, **Sounds** and **Videos**.

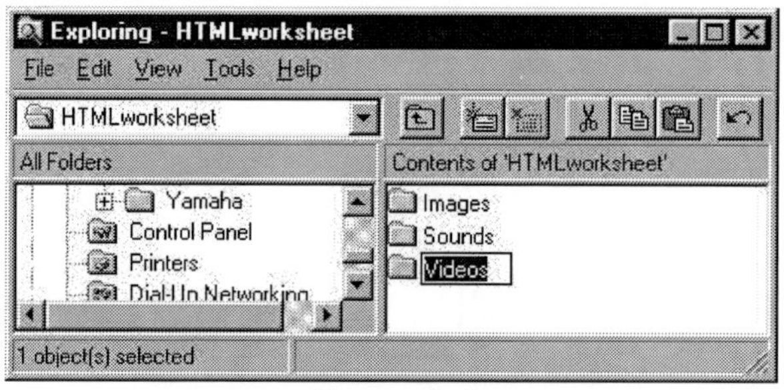

Figure 1.4

Basic HTML Teacher Resources
Worksheet 2B – Writing HTML
Teacher's notes

Topics covered in this worksheet

- Writing code in an editor
- Viewing code in a browser
- Start and end tags
- Parameters and values
- Break tags

This worksheet is intended for additional practice or assessment after Chapter 2 of *Basic HTML* has been completed.
The students should be provided with a copy of *Basic HTML* and a printout of this worksheet, whilst they work through the tasks at the computer. Worksheets should be clearly named so that they can be marked for the answers to the questions.

Teachers may like to ask the students to print their code or, if the class is small enough, their work can be checked straight from the screens.
To add a header to a Notepad file, select **File, Page Setup** from within the Notepad program before printing. Each student will then be able to identify their own work.

Common code errors

- Simple spelling mistakes in parameters, values, file names or code
- Missing start '<' or end '>' brackets
- Putting a space between a parameter and its equals '=' sign
- Forgetting inverted commas "images/pic.jpg" when specifying a file and/or folder
- Although Windows computers use a backslash "\" to separate folders, the Internet is based on the UNIX standard, which uses forward slashes, "/". When specifying images, sounds, videos, links and so on, always use a forward slash to separate folders, e.g. `<A HREF="links/nexpage.html">`
- Forgetting to include the folder as well as the file name in image tags – the files used in *Basic HTML* and this book are generally "relative" files – that is they are named relative to the current directory. For example, if you are writing a page saved as "C:\HTMLworksheet\hello.html" and you want to insert the picture called "C:\HTMLworksheet\images\new\hi.gif", then the code should be `<IMG SRC="images/new/hi.gif">`

It is often helpful for students to write code down on paper before typing it into an editor. Transcription errors may occur, but the act of writing the code down helps some students to consolidate what they have learned, and it is usually easier to concentrate on and understand written words.

When checking code against a master copy, a highlighter pen can help identify any errors or omissions. Highlighting sections of code in both the student's and a master *copy* makes a pattern in which differences can be spotted easily. Keep the original master locked away somewhere safe!

Copy and Paste are extremely useful in minimising the tedium of writing HTML. Encourage the use of them when you consider the students are ready.

If some pupils are not so aware of how to use the Internet or a browser, let them explore www.bbc.co.uk – it is a very large site with many interesting pages and a good navigation system using sensible menus.

Basic HTML
Worksheet 2B – Writing HTML

Student Name:________________________ **Date:**__________________

In worksheets 2 to 5 you are going to make the splash page for a School Charity Web Site. The completed site will look something like Figure 2.1.

Figure 2.1

1. Open a new **Notepad** window from **Start**, **Programs**, **Accessories**, **Notepad** and enter the text shown in Figure 2.2. It is important to indent each section by two spaces more than the previous section so that you can see the structure of the code.

   Wherever the word 'school' is used, change it to the name of your school.

```
<HTML>
  <HEAD>
    <TITLE>Charity Web Site</TITLE>
  </HEAD>

  <BODY>
    <P>
      Welcome to the School Charity Web Site!
    </P>
  </BODY>
</HTML>
```

Figure 2.2

2. Save your work in the folder you made earlier called **HTMLworksheet**. Name the file **splash.html** and remember to set the file type to **All Files** before you press the **Save** button.

3. Load **Windows Explorer** from the **Start** menu and use it to find your **HTMLworksheet** folder. Double-click on your new file, **splash.html**, and a browser window will appear showing your new Charity page.

   Now that you have got everything ready, try to answer the following questions.

4. Write down the tags used to start and end a paragraph.

____

5. Write down the tags used to start and end the `BODY` section of an HTML document.

____

6. Look at your browser window. How is the text "Welcome to the School Charity Web Site!" aligned on the web page at the moment?

____

7. Minimise your browser. In the Notepad window, extend the paragraph tag you have already made by adding the parameter `ALIGN` and the value `CENTER`, as shown in Figure 2.3 below. Then save your code.

```
...
  <BODY>
    <P ALIGN=CENTER>
      Welcome to the School Charity Web site!
    </P>
  </BODY>
...
```

Figure 2.3

8. Which of these **cannot** be the value of the `ALIGN` parameter?

   a) RIGHT ☐

   b) END ☐

   c) LEFT ☐

   d) CENTER ☐

9. Restore your browser window. Which key should you press together with the **Refresh** or **Reload** button to force the browser to load the page again?

   a) SHIFT ☐

   b) ENTER ☐

   c) TAB ☐

   d) F7 ☐

10. Return to Notepad and find the paragraph you just centred. Now add another paragraph below it, so that the body section reads like Figure 2.4.

```
<BODY>
  <P ALIGN=CENTER>
    Welcome to the School Charity Web site!
  </P>
  <P ALIGN=CENTER>
    The School Charity Web Site is about<BR>
    this year's chosen charities,
    how we have raised money for them so far,
    events planned to raise even more
    and
    how you can help!!
  </P>
</BODY>
```

Figure 2.4

11. Save the file and view the page in the browser.

12. Look back at Figure 2.4. A break tag, <BR>, has been used to separate the first new piece of text. Return to Notepad and insert more break tags to make your web page look like Figure 2.5.

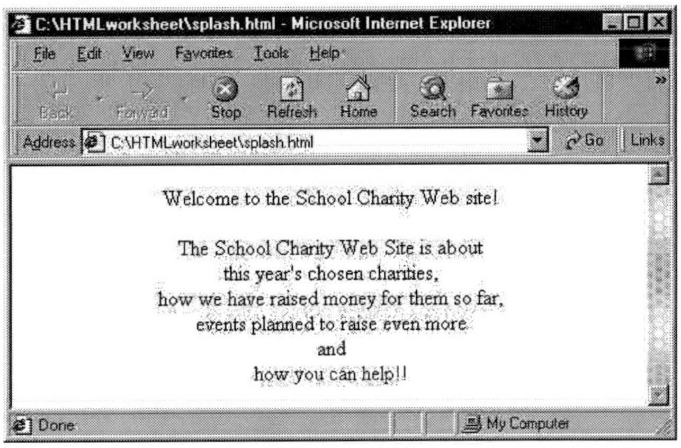

Figure 2.5

In the next session you will be adding some graphics from the Payne-Gallway web site. You need to download them now.

- Connect to the Internet and open <u>www.payne-gallway.co.uk/basichtml/worksheets</u>
- Click on the link called **Images for Charity Web Site: Splash Page**.
- Right-click on the image called **charity-splash.jpg**
- Select **Save Picture As** or **Save Image As** from the drop-down menu and save the file to your **HTMLworksheet**, **Images** folder.
- Save **texture-brushed.jpg** and **purple-bg.jpg** in the same way.
- Disconnect from the Internet.

In most programs, it is possible to save work by holding down the **Control** key (sometimes called **Ctrl**) and tapping the letter **S**. Unfortunately, most versions of Notepad will not recognise this.
It is very inconvenient to have to use the mouse to click on the **File** menu, and then **Save**. You can do exactly the same thing using the keyboard, which is *much* quicker!

- Click inside any Notepad window.

- Hold down the **Alt** key on the keyboard, and tap the **F** key. Then let go of **Alt**. The file menu appears!

- Look carefully at the **File** menu - some of the letters are underlined. For example, **Save** has the letter **S** underlined. Press the letter **S** on your keyboard.

- Your file has just been saved. This is a much quicker way to save than using the mouse - all you do is hold down **Alt** and tap **F**, then let go of **Alt** and tap **S**.

Close all of your work.

Basic HTML Teacher Resources
Worksheet 3B – Graphics and Fonts
Teacher's notes

Topics covered in this worksheet:

- Adding an image to a web page
- Changing the size of an image
- `SIZE` and `FACE` parameters of the `FONT` tag
- Default font size
- Formatting paragraphs to make text stand out

Students' interest in HTML increases greatly once they are able to add their own, or downloaded, images. Varying font faces and sizes also starts to brighten a web page. It is useful to discuss what makes a web page eye-catching or interesting before the session so that they are more focused on the layout and design. There are too many web sites with dreadfully dull fonts and graphics. A little thought and perhaps some rough sketching can make a great difference to the final web page.

A good quality graphics editor such as Adobe Photoshop would allow students to create really interesting and eye-catching headings, such as a smartly designed "Welcome" image and so on. The only important point to remember is that all images must be saved or exported in the JPEG (or GIF) format to be compatible with all modern browsers.
Programs such as Microsoft Paint are very limited and are only included with Windows to give the most basic functionality. Such programs allow students to get into bad habits, and will not produce a very attractive image for the time spent creating it. Graphics are not the main focus of these worksheets, however, so all required images are provided at the Payne-Gallway web site.

Redesigning the pages once the Charity web site is complete would be a really good project for those who are interested.

Basic HTML
Worksheet 3B – Graphics and Fonts

Student Name:________________________ **Date:**____________________

In this worksheet you will start to brighten the splash page using graphics and some different fonts. Visitors will need to know quickly what the web site is about and be excited by the splash page, so that they click and enter your site.

1. Open Notepad (**Start**, **Programs**, **Accessories**, **Notepad**).

2. Select **Open** from the **File** menu and find your Charity **splash.html** file. You won't be able to open the file unless you change the **Files of Type**: option to **All Files (*.*).**

3. Find the two paragraphs you typed in Worksheet 2B and add this paragraph between them.

```
...
  <P ALIGN=CENTER>
    Welcome to the School Charity Web Site!
  </P>
  <P ALIGN=CENTER>
    <IMG SRC="images/charity-splash.jpg">
  </P>
  <P ALIGN=CENTER>
    The School Charity Web Site is about<BR>
...
```

Figure 3.1

4. Save **splash.html** and view it in your browser. It should look very much like Figure 3.2. If it doesn't, then check your code carefully.

Figure 3.2

It is a good idea to include the width and height of the picture in the `<IMG>` tag so that the browser knows how big the image needs to be before loading it. In this way, there will always be enough space for it on the page. You can use any image editor, even a simple one like Paint, to find the width and height of an image.

5. Open Microsoft Paint (**Start**, **Programs**, **Accessories**, **Paint**).

6. Select **Open** from the **File** menu and find your **Images** folder within **HTMLworksheet**.

7. Set the file filter to **All Picture Files** or **All Files**.

8. Select **charity-splash.jpg** and click **Open**.

9. From the **Image** menu, choose **Attributes**.

Figure 3.3

10. What are the width and height of the image? (Make sure that the "Pels" option is selected is there is one)

    Fill in the gaps for the width and height of the charity man:

    `<IMG SRC="images/charity-splash.jpg"` **`WIDTH=___ HEIGHT=___`**`>`

    Now make the `<IMG>` tag in your **splash.html** file look like the tag above.

11. What units is this image measured in? (Pels is just an abbreviation)

    ____

12. Close Paint. (If it asks you whether you would like to save your changes, press **no**.)

13. Will images with the following widths and heights be landscape or portrait orientated?

    a. WIDTH=300, HEIGHT=150 ____________________

    b. WIDTH=300, HEIGHT=400 ____________________

    c. WIDTH=150, HEIGHT=400 ____________________

    d. WIDTH=250, HEIGHT=150 ____________________

The text on the splash page can be changed to make the page more eye-catching and interesting.

14. Click on the Notepad file on the Taskbar to restore your editor.

15. Find the first paragraph in your **splash.html** file and add some font information so that it looks like Figure 3.4.

```
...
  <P ALIGN=CENTER>
    <FONT SIZE=6 FACE="balloon">
      Welcome to the School Charity Web Site!
    </FONT>
  </P>
...
```

Don't worry if you don't have the font called 'balloon' – just use a different one.

Figure 3.4

16. What are the font parameters and values in Figure 3.4?

    Parameter 1__________________ Value 1________________________

    Parameter 2__________________ Value 2________________________

17. Save your code and refresh your browser.

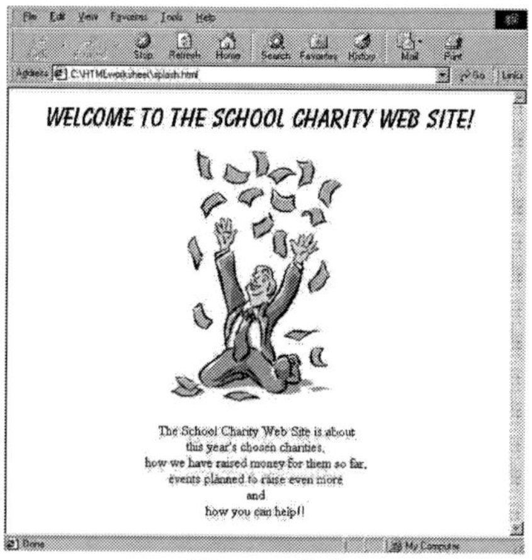

Figure 3.5

18. Find the third paragraph and make the text look like Figure 3.6.

```
...
  <P ALIGN=CENTER>
    <IMG SRC="images/charity-splash.jpg" WIDTH=200 HEIGHT=300>
  </P>
  <P ALIGN=CENTER>
    <FONT FACE="comic sans ms, arial">
      The School Charity Web Site is about<BR>
...
      how you can help!!
    </FONT>
  </P>
...
```

Figure 3.6

19. Read through Figure 3.6 again. What font will appear on a visitor's browser if they don't have 'comic sans ms'?

____

We can make this paragraph stand out by spreading out the text and making some words different sizes.

20. Modify the font properties by making your code look like this:

```
...
  <FONT FACE="comic sans ms, arial" SIZE=3>
     The School Charity Web Site is about<BR>
  </FONT>
  <FONT FACE="comic sans ms, arial" SIZE=4>
    this year's chosen charities,<BR>
    how we have raised money for them so far,<BR>
    events planned to raise even <FONT SIZE=5>more</FONT><BR>
    and<BR>
    how <FONT SIZE=6>you</FONT> can help!!
  </FONT>
...
```

Figure 3.7

21. Font sizes run from 1 to 7. Which is the largest? _______________

22. Place bold tags, <B> and </B>, around the words 'more' and 'you' as in

```
...
  <FONT FACE="comic sans ms, arial" SIZE=3>
    The School Charity Web Site is about<BR>
  </FONT>
  <FONT FACE="comic sans ms, arial" SIZE=4>
    this year's chosen charities,<BR>
    how we have raised money for them so far,<BR>
    events planned to raise even <FONT SIZE=5><B>more</B></FONT><BR>
    and<BR>
    how <FONT SIZE=6><B>you</B></FONT> can help!!
  </FONT>
...
```

Figure 3.8

23. HTML uses the same formatting terms as Word. If <B> makes text bold, what will <I> and <U> do to the text?

<I> ____

<U> ____

Your splash page should look like Figure 3.9.

Figure 3.9

Even if your page does look right, check it against Figure 3.10.

```
<HTML>
  <HEAD>
    <TITLE>Charity Web Site</TITLE>
  </HEAD>
  <BODY>
    <P ALIGN=CENTER>
      <FONT SIZE=6 FACE="balloon bd bt">
        Welcome to the School Charity Web Site!
      </FONT>
    </P>
    <P ALIGN=CENTER>
      <IMG SRC="images/charity-splash.jpg" WIDTH=200 HEIGHT=300>
    </P>
    <P ALIGN=CENTER>
      <FONT FACE="comic sans ms, arial" SIZE=3>
        The School Charity Web Site is about<BR>
      </FONT>
      <FONT FACE="comic sans ms, arial" SIZE=4>
        this year's chosen charities,<BR>
        how we have raised money for them so far,<BR>
        events planned to raise even <FONT SIZE=5><B>more</B></FONT><BR>
        and<BR>
        how <FONT SIZE=6><B>you</B></FONT> can help!!
      </FONT>
    </P>
  </BODY>
</HTML>
```

Figure 3.10

24. Make sure you have saved your web page, then close your work.

Basic HTML Teacher Resources
Worksheet 4B – Colours and Hyperlinks
Teacher's notes

Topics covered in this worksheet

- Practising with colours in HTML
- Preset colours
- Changing the background colour
- Hexadecimal colours
- Adding a simple hyperlink

Colour is one of the joys of writing HTML, but it can be a little daunting to contemplate the hexadecimal system. The preset colours will give students confidence to progress onto using hex. Some students may experiment happily with the entire range of numbers offered by the hex system, however many will be content to use blocks of 00, 77 and FF to start with (where 00 is no colour, 77 is about half way up the brightness scale and FF is full brightness). Get the students to try out various different combinations of red, green and blue to get a feel for colour depth. They should be encouraged to experiment. The **colours.html** file created in this worksheet should help to do this.

Basic HTML
Worksheet 4B – Colours and Hyperlinks

Student Name:____________________ **Date:**________________

In this worksheet you are going to set up an HTML file to experiment with hexadecimal colours.

1. Open a new Notepad window and save it as **colours.html** in your **HTMLworksheet** folder.

2. Type the code in Figure 4.1.and save it.

```
<HTML>
  <HEAD>
    <TITLE>Colours</TITLE>
  </HEAD>
  <BODY BGCOLOR=AQUA>
  </BODY>
</HTML>
```

Figure 4.1

3. Open your browser and look at **colours.html**.

4. In your editor change the value to `TEAL` and save it. Then refresh your browser.

5. Is the background:

   a) Lighter than before ☐

   b) Darker than before ☐

6. HTML colours that have names, like teal and aqua, are called preset colours. Here is a list of the rest of them: `AQUA`, `BLACK`, `BLUE`, `FUCHSIA`, `GRAY`, `GREEN`, `LIME`, `MAROON`, `NAVY`, `OLIVE`, `PURPLE`, `RED`, `SILVER`, `TEAL`, `WHITE` and `YELLOW`. Try some of the others as the background for the page.

7. Make sure you can see **colours.html** in a Notepad window. In the `<BODY>` tag, change the background to `#00FF00`, which is the same as the preset `LIME`.

8. Hexadecimal colours are written by mixing different amounts of red, green and blue. There are 256 shades of red, green or blue colour that can be used to do the mixing. A hexadecimal number in HTML is six digits long. The first two digits say how much red you want in the colour, the second two digits represent green, and the last two digits are for blue. The darkest is written as 00 and the brightest as FF. Lime (#00FF00) is pure green and very bright. Change the green pair to 77. The `<BODY>` tag should now read `<BODY BGCOLOR=#007700>`. Save the file and refresh your browser.

9. Set the value of the blue colour pair to BB, D7, FF or any other hex pair you can think of. Which one looks the worst when you refresh your browser?

10. Norwich City Football Club play in green and yellow. Their rivals, Ipswich Town, play in blue and white. Whose strip do the colours below represent?

`#EEDD00` and `#00DD44` Answer ______________________

11. Type this paragraph just after the `<BODY>` tag. Save it and refresh your browser.

```
...
  <BODY BGCOLOR=#00FFFF>
    <P>
      <FONT SIZE=7>Changing Text Colours</FONT>
    </P>
  </BODY>
</HTML>
```

Figure 4.2

12. What colour is the text in the browser?

____

13. Type `COLOR=BLUE` into the `<FONT>` tag, like this `<FONT COLOR=BLUE size=7>`. Save it and refresh your browser. The text should be a clear royal blue.

14. Set the `BGCOLOR` of the document to `#000000` and the font `COLOR` parameter to `#FFFFFF`. What colour is:

a) the background ______________________

b) the text ______________________

15. Decrease the blue pair of the hexadecimal font colour from `#FFFFBB` to `#FFFF77`, then `#FFFF44`, then `#FFFF00`. Save your page after every change and see what happens to the text colour in your browser.

16. Now close the Notepad window you are using and open **splash.html** again. Add a hyperlink to "homepage.html" at the bottom of your web page so that, once you have made a home page, visitors will be able to get to it from the splash page.
Use the code in Figure 4.3 to add the link, and check that it is there in your browser.

```
...
        how <FONT SIZE=6><B>you</B></FONT> can help!!
      </FONT>
      <BR><A HREF="homepage.html">Click here to enter</A>
    </P>
  </BODY>
</HTML>
```

Figure 4.3

Basic HTML Teacher Resources
Worksheet 5B – Page Layout with Tables
Teacher's notes

Topics covered in this worksheet

- Table, table row and table data tags
- Cell arrangements
- COLSPAN
- ROWSPAN
- Table backgrounds

Tables can be one of the most difficult parts of HTML to grasp. However they are entirely logical and once students understand that they are built up from the 'building blocks' of rows and cells, they become fairly straightforward. Using colour-coded cell backgrounds, the way HTML tables work can be seen quite easily.

It can be helpful if students use Copy and Paste when constructing the more complex tables, however the very simple ones are best typed out in full to get an idea of the layout on a page.

CELLSPACING is the distance between individual cells. CELLPADDING is the distance around the text and other objects *within* each cell. Examples of both are shown below:

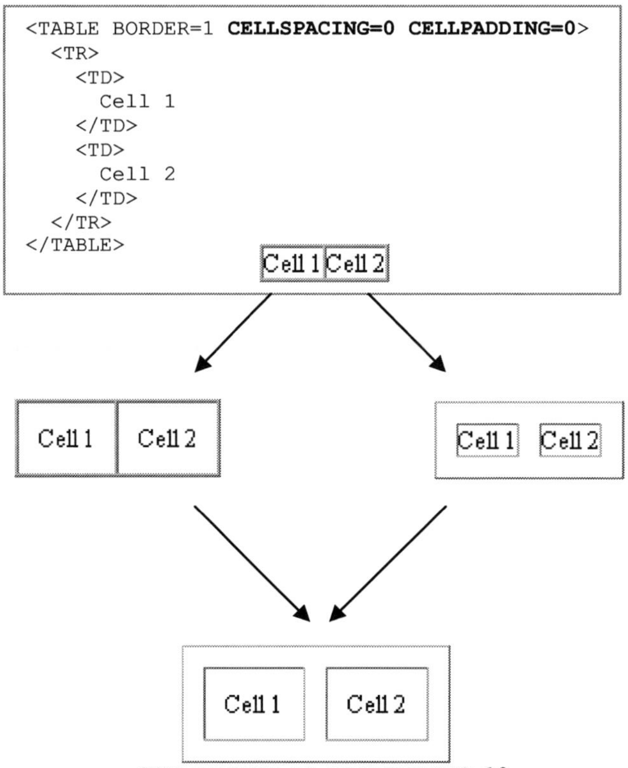

CELLSPACING=0 CELL**PADDING=10**

CELL**SPACING=10** CELLPADDING=0

CELLSPACING=10 CELLPADDING=10

Basic HTML
Worksheet 5B – Page Layout with Tables

Student Name:________________________ **Date:**____________________

In this worksheet you will set up an HTML file to practise different types of tables. Tables are arranged in rows and cells. The practice you do in this worksheet will help you build your home page in the next worksheet and also try different layout in web pages.

```
<HTML>
  <HEAD><TITLE>Tables</TITLE></HEAD>
  <BODY>
    <TABLE BORDER=1>
      <TR>
        <TD>
          Cell A
        </TD>
      </TR>
    </TABLE>
  </BODY>
</HTML>
```

The BORDER parameter is included in the <TABLE> tag so that the cell outline can be seen clearly in your browser.

Figure 5.1

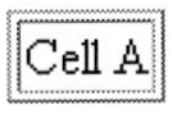

Figure 5.2

Figure 5.1 is the code for Figure 5.2.

1. Which tags start and end a row? ______________ ______________

2. Which tags start and end a cell? ______________ ______________

3. Open a blank new file in Notepad and save it as **tables.html** in your **HTMLworksheet** folder. Don't forget to set the **Save as type** option to **All Files** before you save.

4. Type the code of Figure 5.1 into your **tables.html** file, and then add another cell to the table, as shown in Figure 5.3. Save your changes.

```
...
  <TABLE BORDER=1>
    <TR>
      <TD>
        Cell A
      </TD>
      <TD>
        Cell B
      </TD>
    </TR>
  </TABLE>
...
```

Figure 5.3

Open your **tables.html** file in a browser. Your table should look like this.

Cell A	Cell B

Figure 5.4

There is one row because there is only one set of <TR> and </TR> tags. There are two cells because there are two sets of <TD> and </TD> tags.

5. Put a third cell (call it Cell C) in your **tables.html** file so that your table looks like Figure 5.5 when you refresh your browser.

Cell A	Cell B	Cell C

Figure 5.5

6. Add another row to your table now, but with only one cell (Cell D), as shown in Figure 5.6.

```
...
        Cell B
      </TD>
      <TD>
        Cell C
      </TD>
    </TR>
    <TR>
      <TD>
        Cell D
      </TD>
    </TR>
  </TABLE>
...
```

Figure 5.6

When you refresh your browser, your table should look like this:

Cell A	Cell B	Cell C
Cell D		

Figure 5.7

Because only one cell was added to the second row in your HTML code, there is only one cell (Cell D) in the second row of your table. It is aligned underneath the first cell of the first row (Cell A) so that the table has neatly laid-out columns. This is done automatically by the browser, even though we didn't actually say where Cell D should go along the bottom row.

7. Sometimes, you might want a cell to span across all three columns, like Figure 5.8.

<table>
<tr><td>Cell A</td><td>Cell B</td><td>Cell C</td></tr>
<tr><td colspan="3">Cell D</td></tr>
</table>

Figure 5.8

Add the `COLSPAN` parameter with value **3** to the code for Cell D, as shown in Figure 5.9. Then save your code and see if your table looks like the one above.

```
...
    <TR>
      <TD COLSPAN=3>
        Cell D
      </TD>
    </TR>
  </TABLE>
...
```

Figure 5.9

8. Add an `ALIGN` parameter with value `CENTER` to the paragraph so that the Cell D text is centred.

```
...
    <TR>
      <TD COLSPAN=3 ALIGN=CENTER>
        Cell D
      </TD>
    </TR>
...
```

Figure 5.10

Adding, for example, `ALIGN=CENTER` to a `<TD>` tag will centre *everything* in that cell.
This can also be done by putting a centred paragraph inside the cell.

Does your browser show a table like Figure 5.11?

Cell A	Cell B	Cell C
Cell D		

Figure 5.11

If it doesn't, check your code, make sure you save it and refresh your browser. The entire code for the **tables.html** page should look like this:

```
<HTML>
  <HEAD><TITLE>Tables</TITLE></HEAD>
  <BODY>
    <TABLE BORDER=1>
      <TR>
        <TD>
          Cell A
        </TD>
        <TD>
          Cell B
        </TD>
        <TD>
          Cell C
        </TD>
      </TR>
      <TR>
        <TD COLSPAN=3 ALIGN=CENTER>
          Cell D
        </TD>
      </TR>
    </TABLE>
  </BODY>
</HTML>
```

Figure 5.12

9. Look at Figure 5.13. It is some HTML code for a different table.

```
<TABLE BORDER=1>
  <TR>
    <TD COLSPAN=2>
      <P ALIGN=CENTER>Cell A</P>
    </TD>
  </TR>
  <TR>
    <TD>
      Cell B
    </TD>
    <TD>
      Cell C
    </TD>
  </TR>
</TABLE>
```

Figure 5.13

Which of these does the code in Figure 5.13 correspond to?

A

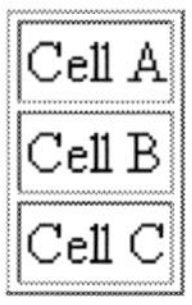

B

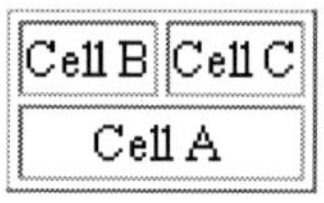

C

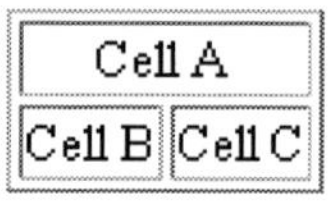

D

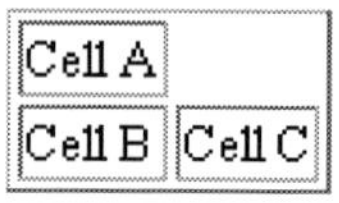

Answer __________

10. The `ROWSPAN` parameter makes a cell stretch over however many rows you like. It is just like the `COLSPAN` parameter, but works vertically instead of horizontally.

Figure 5.14 shows how to merge rows in a simple table:

```
<TABLE BORDER=1>
  <TR>
    <TD ROWSPAN=2>
      Cell A
    </TD>
    <TD>
      Cell B
    </TD>
  </TR>
  <TR>
    <TD>
      Cell C
    </TD>
  </TR>
</TABLE>
```

There are two cells in the first row, Cell A and Cell B. Cell A is merged downwards across two rows because it has the **ROWSPAN=2** parameter

There only needs to be one cell in the second row because Cell A has been merged downwards to fill up the rest of the space.

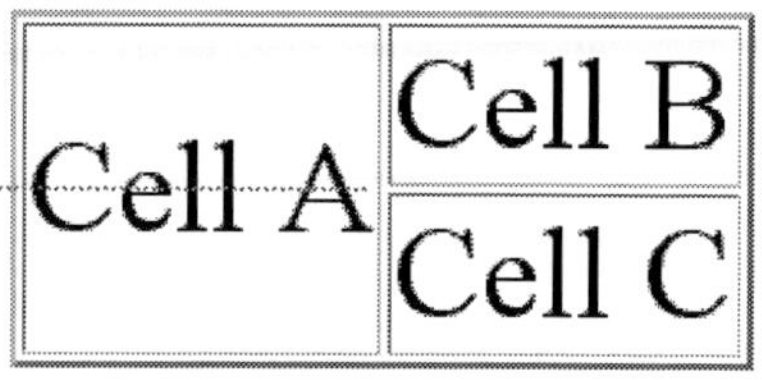

Figure 5.14

11. Look at Figure 5.15 closely. Work out which cell will be merged downwards. (This is quite a tricky question so you will have to think!)

```
<TABLE BORDER=1>
  <TR>
    <TD>
      Cell A
    </TD>
    <TD ROWSPAN=2>
      Cell B
    </TD>
    <TD>
      Cell C
    </TD>
  </TR>
  <TR>
    <TD>
      Cell D
    </TD>
    <TD>
      Cell E
    </TD>
  </TR>
</TABLE>
```

Figure 5.15

Which table will be produced by the code in Figure 5.15?

A

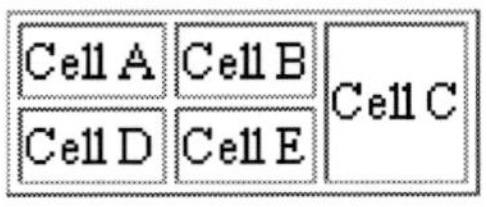

B

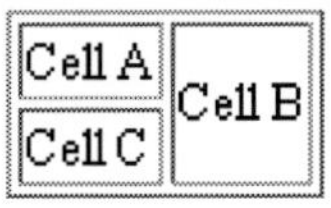

C

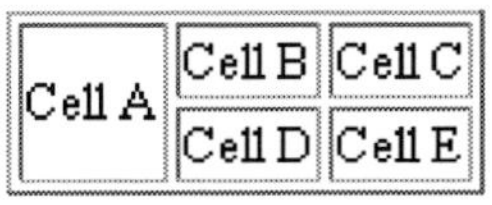

D

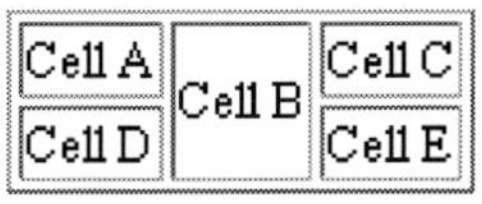

Answer ____________

12. In the space at the foot of the page, write the HTML code for this table.

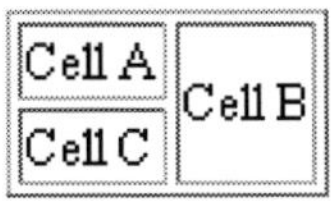

13. Tables can be coloured to achieve different effects. Edit your code so that it is the same as Figure 5.16. Straight away you will see how much smarter the table looks by just having a line border instead the standard raised one.

```
<HTML>
  <HEAD><TITLE>Tables</TITLE></HEAD>
  <BODY BGCOLOR=WHITE TEXT=WHITE>
    <TABLE BORDER=0 BGCOLOR=WHITE CELLSPACING=1 CELLPADDING=3>
      <TR>
        <TD BGCOLOR=#0000AA>
          Cell A
        </TD>
        <TD BGCOLOR=#0000CC>
          Cell B
        </TD>
        <TD BGCOLOR=#0000EE>
          Cell C
        </TD>
      </TR>
      <TR>
        <TD COLSPAN=3 ALIGN=CENTER BGCOLOR=#990099>
          Cell D
        </TD>
      </TR>
    </TABLE>
  </BODY>
</HTML>
```

Removing the standard table border by adding BORDER=0 to the <TABLE> tag makes everything look tidier.

Figure 5.16

Play around with different colours to find a colour scheme that you really like.

14. In the <TABLE> tag, change CELLSPACING=1 to CELLSPACING=0 and have a look in your browser. It actually makes quite a big difference to the look of the table.

At last, it's time to put some tables into your splash page to give it a proper layout.

15. Save **tables.html** and then select **Open** from the **File** and load **splash.html**. Once you have done that, open **splash.html** in your browser as well.

16. Carefully add everything in bold from Figure 5.17 to your own **splash.html** file. Don't forget to indent all the other lines of code you have written so that the entire file stays tidy and readable.

    Make sure you keep checking how the page looks in a browser whilst you are making these bigger changes.

```
<HTML>
  <HEAD>
    <TITLE>Charity Web Site</TITLE>
  </HEAD>
  <BODY BGCOLOR=WHITE>
    <TABLE WIDTH=500 CELLPADDING=3 CELLSPACING=0 BORDER=0 ALIGN=CENTER>
      <TR>
        <TD ALIGN=CENTER BGCOLOR=PURPLE>
          <FONT SIZE=5 FACE="comic sans ms" COLOR=WHITE>
            Welcome to the School Charity Web Site!
          </FONT>
        </TD>
      </TR>
      <TR>
        <TD ALIGN=CENTER BACKGROUND="images/purple-bg.jpg">
          <IMG SRC="images/charity-splash.jpg" WIDTH=200 HEIGHT=300><BR>
          <FONT FACE="comic sans ms, arial" SIZE=3 COLOR=PURPLE>
            The School Charity Web Site is about<BR>
          </FONT>
          <FONT FACE="comic sans ms, arial" SIZE=4 COLOR=PURPLE>
            this year's chosen charities,<BR>
            how we have raised money for them so far,<BR>
            events planned to raise even <FONT SIZE=5><B>more</B></FONT><BR>
            and<BR>
            how <FONT SIZE=6><B>you</B></FONT> can help!!
          </FONT>
          <BR><A HREF="homepage.html">Click here to enter</A>
        </TD>
      </TR>
    </TABLE>
  </BODY>
</HTML>
```

Because everything is now inside <TD> tags aligned to the centre, there is no need to keep the <P> tags any longer. You can delete them from your code so that your page looks just like Figure 5.17.

Figure 5.17

17. And for the last step, add another table around the outside of the one you just made, as shown in Figure 5.18. This process is called "nesting" tables.

```
...
  </HEAD>
  <BODY BACKGROUND="images/texture-brushed.jpg">

    <TABLE CELLPADDING=1 CELLSPACING=0 BORDER=0 ALIGN=CENTER BGCOLOR=PURPLE><TR><TD>

      <TABLE WIDTH=500 CELLPADDING=3 CELLSPACING=0 BORDER=0 ALIGN=CENTER>
        <TR>
          <TD ALIGN=CENTER BGCOLOR=PURPLE>
            <FONT SIZE=5 FACE="comic sans ms" COLOR=WHITE>
              Welcome to the School Charity Web Site!
...
            </FONT>
            <BR><A HREF="homepage.html">Click here to enter</A>
          </TD>
        </TR>
      </TABLE>

    </TD></TR></TABLE>

  </BODY>
</HTML>
```

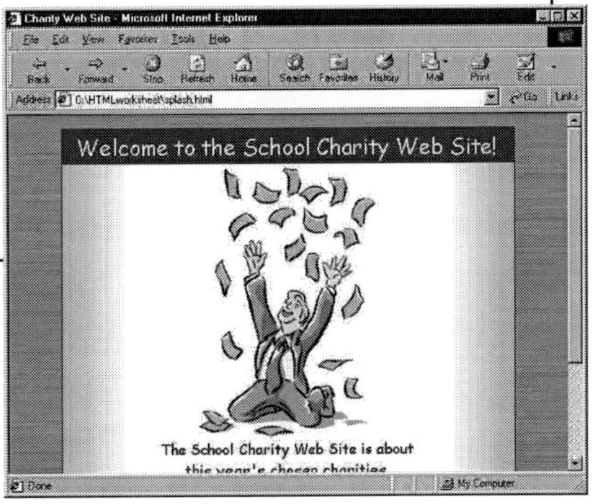

Figure 5.18

18. Save your work and see how it looks!

Basic HTML Teacher Resources
Worksheet 6B – Building your Home Page
Teacher's notes

Topics covered in this worksheet

- Starting a home page
- Creating links to the rest of the site
- Hyperlink colour conventions
- Using tables to arrange the page

Colour and table layout will brighten up a web page. Students may be reluctant to make the intellectual jump needed to see a web page in terms of tables. The use of pencil and paper to sketch out their pages before committing them to code should help them.

The 'fine tuning' of the page layout may seem unnecessary; however students should be encouraged to look at their web pages critically. Subtle little details can make quite a difference to the final appeal of the page. Conversely, too much overt detail can turn visitors away! 'Keep it simple' is probably the best maxim, but keeping a critical eye out for delicate amendments is also crucial to the look of the final piece of work.

Basic HTML
Worksheet 6B – Building your Home Page

Student Name:______________________ **Date:_________________**

In this worksheet you will use the work you have done on colours and tables to produce an attractive home page.

The home page and the other three pages will have the page layout shown in Figure 6.1. There are two tables: one simple table at the top with two cells on the same row, and then a more complex table below it. Once you have finished it, you should have something that looks a bit like Figure 6.2.

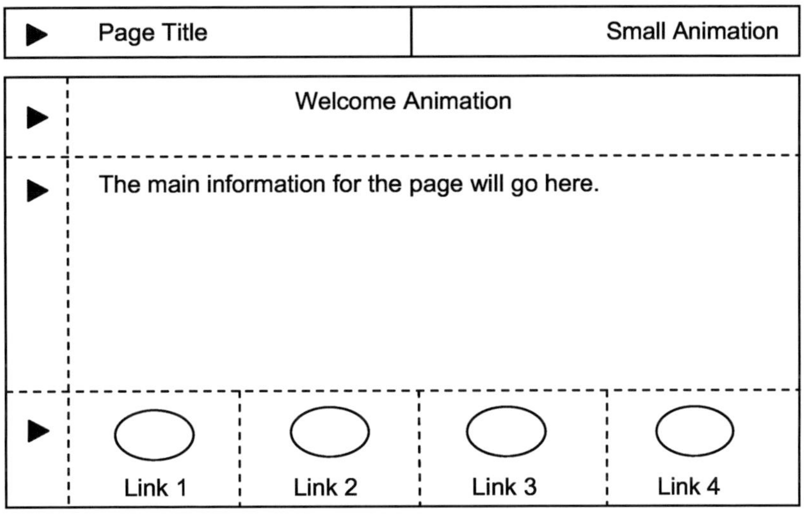

Figure 6.1

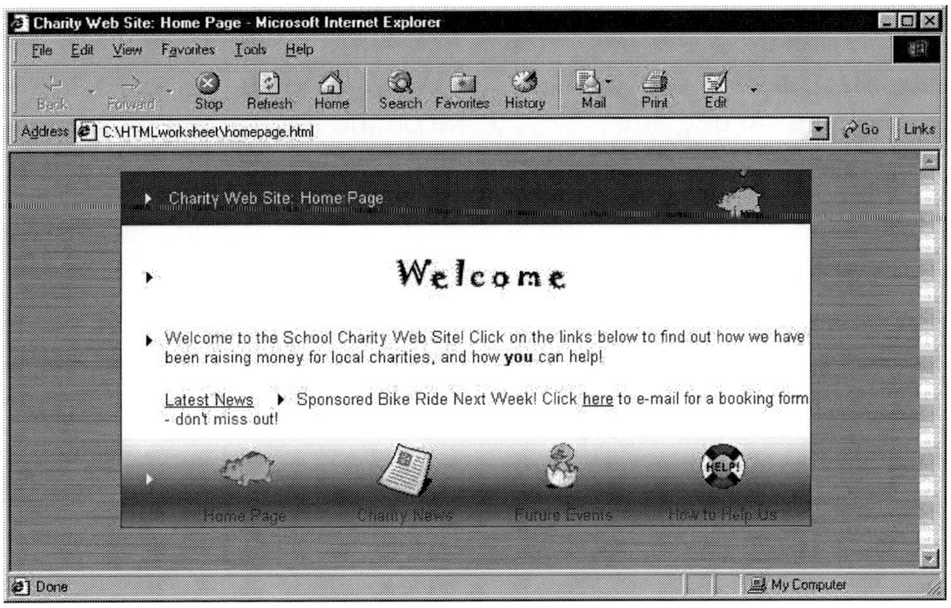

Figure 6.2

In total there will be five pages in this web site – the splash page, the home page, and three others: **charitynews.html**, **futureevents.html** and **howtohelp.html**. You will create those in the next worksheet.

1. Now that you know the names of all the pages that will be part of this site, draw a web site plan in the space below.

2. Connect to the Internet and log on to
www.payne-gallway.co.uk/basichtml/worksheets

   Click on the link **Images for Charity Web Site: Home Page**, and download all of the image files by right-clicking on each picture and selecting **Save Image As** or **Save Picture As** from the popup menu. Save them to your **HTMLworksheet**, **Images** folder.

3. Disconnect from the Internet and close your browser. Open **Windows Explorer** from **Programs** in the **Start** menu and go into the **Images** folder inside **HTMLworksheet**. You should have all of these files:

   black-arrow.gif, blank.gif, button1.gif, button2.gif, button3.gif, button4.gif, charity-splash.jpg, money-pig.gif, purple-bg.jpg, purple-fade.jpg, texture-brushed.jpg, white-arrow.jpg.

4. Minimise Windows Explorer, then open a new Notepad window and type in the code from Figure 6.3.

   Notice that the `<HTML>`, `<HEAD>` and `<TITLE>` tags are all on the same line – tags can be arranged any way you like on the page. You only really need to indent when you are using code that is more complicated and that you are not so used to. Follow the way that the code is arranged throughout this worksheet so that you can clearly see what is happening, and also make the HTML code easier to read.

```
<HTML><HEAD><TITLE>Charity Web Site: Home Page</TITLE></HEAD>
  <BODY BACKGROUND="images/texture-brushed.jpg" TEXT=#303030>
    <TABLE WIDTH=560 CELLPADDING=0 CELLSPACING=0 BORDER=1
                                        ALIGN=CENTER BGCOLOR=PURPLE>
      <TR>
        <TD ALIGN=LEFT>
          <IMG SRC="images/white-arrow.gif">
          <FONT COLOR=WHITE FACE="arial" SIZE=2>Charity Web Site: Home Page</FONT>
        </TD>
        <TD ALIGN=RIGHT>
          <IMG SRC="images/money-pig.gif" WIDTH=40 HEIGHT=40>
          <IMG SRC="images/blank.gif" WIDTH=30 HEIGHT=1>
        </TD>
      </TR>
    </TABLE>
  </BODY>
</HTML>
```

Figure 6.3

5. Save what you have just typed as **homepage.html** in the **HTMLworksheet** folder. Set **Save As Type** to **All Files** before you save.

6. View the page in a browser. Does it look like the top of Figure 6.2? It should do! The most important thing is that you understand how the table works. Take a couple of minutes to look through your code and see why it appears in the browser the way it does.

7. Now add another table beneath it, but before the <BODY> tag, like this:

```
...
          <IMG SRC="images/blank.gif" WIDTH=30 HEIGHT=1>
        </TD>
      </TR>
    </TABLE>

    <TABLE WIDTH=560 CELLPADDING=0 CELLSPACING=0 BORDER=1 ALIGN=CENTER
                                                          BGCOLOR=WHITE>
      <TR>
        <TD ALIGN=CENTER VALIGN=MIDDLE><IMG SRC="images/black-arrow.gif"></TD>
        <TD HEIGHT=50 ALIGN=CENTER>
          Welcome
        </TD>
      </TR>
      <TR>
        <TD ALIGN=CENTER VALIGN=TOP><IMG SRC="images/black-arrow.gif"></TD>
        <TD VALIGN=TOP>
          <FONT FACE="arial" SIZE=2>
            <P>
              Welcome to the School Charity Web Site!
              Click on the links below to find out how we have been raising
              money for local charities, and how <B>you</B> can help!
            </P>
            <P>
              <U>Latest News</U><IMG SRC="images/black-arrow.gif">
              Sponsored Bike Ride Next Week!
              Click <A HREF="mailto:booking@school.co.uk">here</A> to e-mail
              for a booking form - don't miss out!
            </P>
          </FONT>
        </TD>
      </TR>
    </TABLE>
  </BODY>
</HTML>
```

Type it slowly and carefully so that you don't have to spend a long time trying to find out why the page doesn't look right!

Figure 6.4

8. If you haven't made any mistakes, your page should look like this:

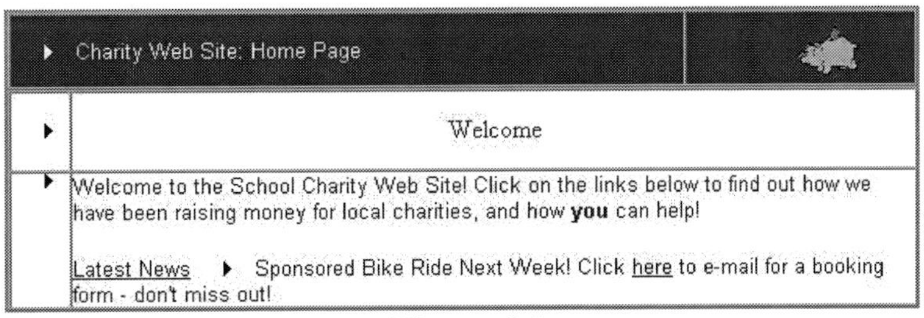

Figure 6.5

9. The HTML file is already quite complicated, so you need some way to keep track of where everything is in your code. What are the tags called that allow you to label various parts of an HTML document?

___

10. Write an example of one of the tags from Question 9 here:

___

11. In some of the cells you created, the `VALIGN` parameter is used. It can have one of three values: `TOP`, `MIDDLE` (which is the default) or `BOTTOM`. For example, `VALIGN=TOP` moves everything inside the cell upwards so it gets as close as possible to the top of the cell.

    What does the `ALIGN` parameter of the `<TD>` tag do?

___

___

12. Add another row to the bottom of the second table, as shown below. This row will have five cells – the first one for a little arrow, and the other four for the links to other pages.

```
...
              for a booking form - don't miss out!
            </P>
          </FONT>
        </TD>
      </TR>
      <TR>
        <TD BACKGROUND="images/purple-fade.jpg" VALIGN=MIDDLE>
          <IMG SRC="images/white-arrow.gif">
        </TD>
        <TD WIDTH=130 BACKGROUND="images/purple-fade.jpg" ALIGN=CENTER>
          <IMG SRC="images/button1.gif" ALIGN=MIDDLE><BR>
          <FONT SIZE=2 FACE="arial">Home Page</FONT>
        </TD>
        <TD WIDTH=130 BACKGROUND="images/purple-fade.jpg" ALIGN=CENTER>
          <IMG SRC="images/button2.gif" ALIGN=MIDDLE><BR>
          <FONT SIZE=2 FACE="arial">Charity News</FONT>
        </TD>
        <TD WIDTH=130 BACKGROUND="images/purple-fade.jpg" ALIGN=CENTER>
          <IMG SRC="images/button3.gif" ALIGN=MIDDLE><BR>
          <FONT SIZE=2 FACE="arial">Future Events</FONT>
        </TD>
        <TD WIDTH=130 BACKGROUND="images/purple-fade.jpg" ALIGN=CENTER>
          <IMG SRC="images/button4.gif" ALIGN=MIDDLE><BR>
          <FONT SIZE=2 FACE="arial">How to Help Us</FONT>
        </TD>
      </TR>
    </TABLE>
  </BODY>
</HTML>
```

Figure 6.6

13. Save your work and refresh your browser. The page has suddenly gone terribly wrong!

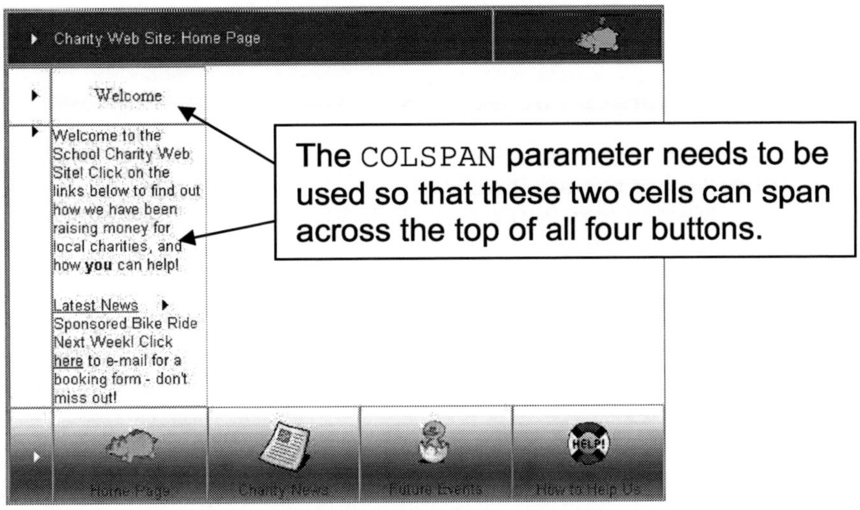

Figure 6.7

14. Use Figure 6.8 to help you find where to add the two COLSPAN=4 parameters.

```
...
  <TR>
    <TD ALIGN=CENTER VALIGN=MIDDLE><IMG SRC="images/black-arrow.gif"></TD>
    <TD HEIGHT=50 ALIGN=CENTER COLSPAN=4>
      Welcome
    </TD>
  </TR>
  <TR>
    <TD ALIGN=CENTER VALIGN=TOP><IMG SRC="images/black-arrow.gif"></TD>
    <TD VALIGN=TOP COLSPAN=4>
      <FONT FACE="arial" SIZE=2>
        <P>
          Welcome to the School Charity Web Site!
          Click on the links below to find out how we have been raising
...
```

Figure 6.8

15. Save **homepage.html** again and then refresh your browser. The page should look much better. Now that you can see the final layout of the tables, the grey borders can be removed. In both of the table tags, change BORDER=1 into BORDER=0 and have a look in your browser - the page is transformed.

16. At the moment the icons at the foot of the page don't do anything. You need to add hyperlinks by placing <A> tags around the images. Check your code against Figure 6.9 if you get stuck.

```
...
  <TD BACKGROUND="images/purple-fade.jpg" VALIGN=MIDDLE>
    <IMG SRC="images/white-arrow.gif">
  </TD>
  <TD WIDTH=130 BACKGROUND="images/purple-fade.jpg" ALIGN=CENTER>
    <A HREF="homepage.html">
      <IMG SRC="images/button1.gif" ALIGN=MIDDLE BORDER=0><BR>
    </A>
    <FONT SIZE=2 FACE="arial">Home Page</FONT>
  </TD>
  <TD WIDTH=130 BACKGROUND="images/purple-fade.jpg" ALIGN=CENTER>
    <A HREF="charitynews.html">
      <IMG SRC="images/button2.gif" ALIGN=MIDDLE BORDER=0><BR>
    </A>
    <FONT SIZE=2 FACE="arial">Charity News</FONT>
  </TD>
  <TD WIDTH=130 BACKGROUND="images/purple-fade.jpg" ALIGN=CENTER>
    <A HREF="futureevents.html">
      <IMG SRC="images/button3.gif" ALIGN=MIDDLE BORDER=0><BR>
    </A>
    <FONT SIZE=2 FACE="arial">Future Events</FONT>
  </TD>
  <TD WIDTH=130 BACKGROUND="images/purple-fade.jpg" ALIGN=CENTER>
    <A HREF="howtohelp.html">
      <IMG SRC="images/button4.gif" ALIGN=MIDDLE BORDER=0><BR>
    </A>
    <FONT SIZE=2 FACE="arial">How to Help Us</FONT>
...
```

Figure 6.9

17. Add some comments to your code so that, when you come back to it another time, you can easily find where everything is.

```
...
      <TD ALIGN=LEFT>
        <IMG SRC="images/white-arrow.gif">
<!-- page title -->
        <FONT COLOR=WHITE FACE="arial" SIZE=2>Charity Web Site: Home Page</FONT>
      </TD>
...
      <TD ALIGN=CENTER VALIGN=MIDDLE><IMG SRC="images/black-arrow.gif"></TD>
      <TD HEIGHT=50 ALIGN=CENTER COLSPAN=4>
<!-- welcome -->
        Welcome
...
        <FONT FACE="arial" SIZE=2>
<!-- main text -->
          <P>
            Welcome to the School Charity Web Site!
...
        <A HREF="homepage.html">
<!-- first button -->
          <IMG SRC="images/button1.gif" ALIGN=MIDDLE BORDER=0><BR>
...
        <A HREF="charitynews.html">
<!-- second button -->
          <IMG SRC="images/button2.gif" ALIGN=MIDDLE BORDER=0><BR>
...
        <A HREF="futureevents.html">
<!-third button -->
          <IMG SRC="images/button3.gif" ALIGN=MIDDLE BORDER=0><BR>
...
        <A HREF="howtohelp.html">
<!-- fourth button -->
          <IMG SRC="images/button4.gif" ALIGN=MIDDLE BORDER=0><BR>
...
```

Figure 6.10

18. Finally, lets put a purple border around the second table so that the page looks tidier. Do this by creating another table outside the second table.

    What is the process called when one table is placed inside another?

    ____

19. Add the bold code in Figure 6.11 to your **homepage.html** file:

```
          <IMG SRC="images/money-pig.gif" WIDTH=40 HEIGHT=40>
          <IMG SRC="images/blank.gif" WIDTH=30 HEIGHT=1>
        </TD>
      </TR>
    </TABLE>

    <TABLE CELLPADDING=1 CELLSPACING=0 BORDER=0 BGCOLOR=PURPLE ALIGN=CENTER><TR><TD>

    <TABLE WIDTH=560 CELLPADDING=0 CELLSPACING=0 BORDER=0 ALIGN=CENTER BGCOLOR=WHITE>
      <TR>
        <TD ALIGN=CENTER VALIGN=MIDDLE><IMG SRC="images/black-arrow.gif"></TD>
        <TD HEIGHT=50 ALIGN=CENTER COLSPAN=4>
<!-- welcome -->
          Welcome
...
        <TD WIDTH=130 BACKGROUND="images/purple-fade.jpg" ALIGN=CENTER>
          <A HREF="howtohelp.html">
<!-- fourth button -->
            <IMG SRC="images/button4.gif" ALIGN=MIDDLE BORDER=0><BR>
          </A>
          <FONT SIZE=2 FACE="arial">How to Help Us</FONT>
        </TD>
      </TR>
    </TABLE>

    </TD></TR></TABLE>

  </BODY>
</HTML>
```

Figure 6.11

20. Save your file and refresh the browser. If you look carefully, the purple border has made the bottom table wider than the top table, so change the width of the top table from 560 to 562 pixels.

```
<HTML><HEAD><TITLE>Charity Web Site: Home Page</TITLE></HEAD>
  <BODY BACKGROUND="images/texture-brushed.jpg" TEXT=#303030>
    <TABLE WIDTH=562 CELLPADDING=0 CELLSPACING=0 BORDER=0
                                              ALIGN=CENTER BGCOLOR=PURPLE>
      <TR>
        <TD ALIGN=LEFT>
          <IMG SRC="images/white-arrow.gif">
<!-- page title -->
...
```

Figure 6.12

21. Save **homepage.html** and, once you have checked in the browser, close your work.

Basic HTML Teacher Resources
Worksheet 7B – Multimedia
Teacher's notes

Topics covered in this worksheet

- Sound Files
- Copying HTML files
- Flash Animations
- JavaScript

The basic use of sound files, as described in *Basic HTML* is put into practice again here.

Flash animations are covered here instead of Applets, because some newer Microsoft browsers do not support Java. According to Microsoft, it has been found more useful as a server tool, rather that its use in Applets for web pages. Unfortunately this means that millions of web pages around the world will not work properly any more.

Java is a superbly powerful tool, and it is well worth learning how to use it, or even learning programming with it because it is free to download the SDK (Software Development Kit) and many code, or graphical editors. Java is not just a pretty toy – it is a full programming language, infinitely more powerful than HTML.
Flash, on the other hand, is purely for animation. It does this very well however, and should be promoted. It is very expensive to create Flash animations using the professional quality design program, but there is a free version that lets you make "text-only" animations – ones that can have all sorts of text effects, but not pictures. See www.payne-gallway.co.uk/basichtml/worksheets for more information. For Flash animations to work, the Flash Plugin must be enabled. Go to www.macromedia.com/flash if the example on this worksheet does not work. Most browsers do come with the plugin installed already, however.

Lastly, JavaScript does really have much to do with Java – it is a simple addition to HTML that allows some extra effects to be included in a web page.

Basic HTML
Worksheet 7B – Multimedia

Student Name:________________________ **Date:**__________________

1. Go to www.payne-gallway.co.uk/basichtml/worksheets and click on the **Multimedia** link.

2. Right-click on the link called **ching.wav** and select **Save Link As** or **Save Target As** from the popup menu.

3. Save the file to the **Sounds** folder inside **HTMLworksheet**.

4. Now right-click the **welcome.swf** link and, in the same way, save it to the **Videos** folder you made inside **HTMLworksheet**.

5. Now download the four button pictures, **button1-new.gif**, **button2-new.gif**, **button3-new.gif**, and **button4-new.gif** by right-clicking on each picture and selecting **Save Picture As** or **Save Image As**. Save them to the **Images** folder inside **HTMLworksheet**.

6. Disconnect from the Internet.

7. Open a new Notepad window and load **homepage.html** from the **HTMLworksheet** folder. Scroll down to the bottom of the window and, just before the </BODY> tag, add this code:

```
...
          <FONT SIZE=2 FACE="arial">How to Help Us</FONT>
        </TD>
      </TR>
    </TABLE>

    </TD></TR></TABLE>

    <EMBED SRC="sounds/ching.wav" AUTOSTART=TRUE LOOP=FALSE
                                             WIDTH=1 HEIGHT=1>
    </EMBED>
  </BODY>
</HTML>
```

Figure 7.1

8. Look in the bottom-right corner of your screen. There should be icon that looks like this  or like this . Click once on the icon, and a box should appear.

9. Change it so that it looks like this: 

Click somewhere else on the screen for the box to disappear. The icon should now look like this: .

10. Open **homepage.html** in a browser. If you have loudspeakers connected to your computer, you should hear the "*ching*" when the page loads.

The easiest way to create the other three pages in this web site is to copy the home page three times. You can either do this using Windows Explorer, or using Notepad. We will use Notepad here.

11. Make sure you have **homepage.html** (from your **HTMLworksheet** folder) in a Notepad window.

12. Select **Save As...** from the **File** menu.

    - Make sure the **Save In:** box is showing your **HTMLworksheet** folder.
    - Change the file name to **charitynews.html**.
    - Set the file type to **All Files (*.*)**.
    - Press **Save**.

13. Now do exactly the same thing two more times. Firstly save the page as **futureevents.html** and then as **howtohelp.html**.

14. Select **Open** from the **File** menu and load **homepage.html** again. It's time to add some Flash!

15. Replace the word "Welcome" with the bold code in Figure 7.2.

```
...
    <TR>
      <TD ALIGN=CENTER VALIGN=MIDDLE><IMG SRC="images/black-arrow.gif"></TD>
      <TD HEIGHT=80 ALIGN=CENTER COLSPAN=4>
<!-- welcome -->
        <EMBED SRC="videos/welcome.swf" WIDTH=200 HEIGHT=80 AUTOSTART=TRUE>
        </EMBED>
      </TD>
    </TR>
...
```

Figure 7.2

16. Save the page, and view it in your browser. Watch the animation!

17. Now that the home page is all done, go through your other pages and change the titles and the information. Talk to your teacher and see if your School has been involved in any charity events lately that you could write about. If not, make some up!

JavaScript was invented as an extension to HTML. As you have seen so far, you can't animate anything in HTML itself, you have to use other objects to provide sound, video and anything else. Add some JavaScript, and you can do all sorts of clever things.
Read through the next few questions very carefully.

18. Make sure you have a Notepad window on the screen showing **homepage.html**.

19. The reason you downloaded the extra buttons at the start of this worksheet (**button1-new.gif** and so on) is because they are slightly brighter versions of the buttons you have already used.
Using JavaScript, you can make the new buttons appear when the mouse is moved over the top of the ones you have at the moment.

First of all, tell JavaScript all the images that it needs to use. Use the `<SCRIPT>` tag to start the JavaScript code.

```
<HTML><HEAD><TITLE>Charity Web Site: Home Page</TITLE></HEAD>

  <SCRIPT LANGUAGE="JavaScript1.1">
  </SCRIPT>

  <BODY BACKGROUND="images/texture-brushed.jpg" TEXT=#303030>
    <TABLE WIDTH=562 CELLPADDING=0 CELLSPACING=0 BORDER=0
...
```

This code tells the browser which version of JavaScript to use.

The `<SCRIPT>` tag can go outside the body of the document because it doesn't need to display anything yet.

Figure 7.3

Then add eight JavaScript images – four for the normal buttons, and four for the brighter buttons:

```
...
  <SCRIPT LANGUAGE="JavaScript1.1">
    icon1=new Image();  icon1.src='images/button1.gif';
    icon1b=new Image(); icon1b.src='images/button1-new.gif';
    icon2=new Image();  icon2.src='images/button2.gif';
    icon2b=new Image(); icon2b.src='images/button2-new.gif';
    icon3=new Image();  icon3.src='images/button3.gif';
    icon3b=new Image(); icon3b.src='images/button3-new.gif';
    icon4=new Image();  icon4.src='images/button4.gif';
    icon4b=new Image(); icon4b.src='images/button4-new.gif';
  </SCRIPT>
...
```

Notice how JavaScript also uses the word **src** to ask where to find an image.

Each JavaScript command ends with a semicolon ";"

JavaScript lets each image have a name. For example, we are calling the first button **icon1**, and the brighter first button **icon1b**.
The same goes for the other images.

Figure 7.4

20. Now that JavaScript knows what to load, we can tell it where to find the buttons on the page.

Add NAME parameters to the <IMG> tags so your JavaScript code can see where the buttons are on the layout of the page.

```
...
  <IMG SRC="images/button1.gif" ALIGN=MIDDLE BORDER=0 NAME="i1"><BR>
...
  <IMG SRC="images/button2.gif" ALIGN=MIDDLE BORDER=0 NAME="i2"><BR>
...
  <IMG SRC="images/button3.gif" ALIGN=MIDDLE BORDER=0 NAME="i3"><BR>
...
  <IMG SRC="images/button4.gif" ALIGN=MIDDLE BORDER=0 NAME="i4"><BR>
...
```

Figure 7.5

21. Now for the JavaScript instructions. They make lots of sense – the **`OnMouseOver`** instruction will be run when you move the mouse over a link. For example, when you move the mouse over the first link, JavaScript will display the brighter version of the picture.

    When you move the mouse away from the button, the **`OnMouseOut`** command is run, and JavaScript will put the image back to normal.

    Where you see the word **`document`** in Figure 7.6, it means JavaScript is going to do something to change the look of the current document, **homepage.html**.

```
...
        <TD WIDTH=130 BACKGROUND="images/purple-fade.jpg" ALIGN=CENTER>
          <A HREF="homepage.html" onmouseover="document.i1.src=icon1b.src;"
                                  onmouseout="document.i1.src=icon1.src;">
<!-- first button -->
            <IMG SRC="images/button1.gif" ALIGN=MIDDLE BORDER=0 NAME="i1"><BR>
          </A>
          <FONT SIZE=2 FACE="arial">Home Page</FONT>
        </TD>
        <TD WIDTH=130 BACKGROUND="images/purple-fade.jpg" ALIGN=CENTER>
          <A HREF="charitynews.html" onmouseover="document.i2.src=icon2b.src;"
                                     onmouseout="document.i2.src=icon2.src;">
<!-- second button -->
            <IMG SRC="images/button2.gif" ALIGN=MIDDLE BORDER=0 NAME="i2"><BR>
          </A>
          <FONT SIZE=2 FACE="arial">Charity News</FONT>
        </TD>
        <TD WIDTH=130 BACKGROUND="images/purple-fade.jpg" ALIGN=CENTER>
          <A HREF="futureevents.html" onmouseover="document.i3.src=icon3b.src;"
                                      onmouseout="document.i3.src=icon3.src;">
<!-third button -->
            <IMG SRC="images/button3.gif" ALIGN=MIDDLE BORDER=0 NAME="i3"><BR>
          </A>
          <FONT SIZE=2 FACE="arial">Future Events</FONT>
        </TD>
        <TD WIDTH=130 BACKGROUND="images/purple-fade.jpg" ALIGN=CENTER>
          <A HREF="howtohelp.html" onmouseover="document.i4.src=icon4b.src;"
                                   onmouseout="document.i4.src=icon4.src;">
<!-- fourth button -->
            <IMG SRC="images/button4.gif" ALIGN=MIDDLE BORDER=0 NAME="i4"><BR>
...
```

Don't forget to close each <A> tag after the `OnMouseOut` commands!

Figure 7.6

Save your file and refresh your browser. The buttons appear to be highlighted when you move the mouse over them. If it doesn't work, check that JavaScript is enabled in your browser.

This is how the code works:

```
onmouseover="document.i1.src=icon1b.src;
```

When the mouse is moved over the link, the source of the `<IMG>` tag with the name **i1** is changed to the source of the JavaScript image called **icon1b**.

22. If you like the effect, change all the other pages so that they use JavaScript as well. Go to www.payne-gallway.co.uk/basichtml/worksheets/complete to see the finished site. Check that yours is correct!

Basic HTML Teacher Resources
Worksheet 8B – Uploading by FTP
Teacher's notes

Topics covered in this worksheet

- The FTP Service
- Security

At a personal or small business level, FTP is a very secure way to publish a web site. Although there are a dwindling number of good free servers around, there are some really good packages available.

Visit www.payne-gallway.co.uk/basichtml/worksheets for some recommended options.

The best way to allow an entire class to experience uploading their web sites seems to be for the teacher to create *one* account on a free server, and on it, create a folder for each pupil. In this way, the service provider does not have to give away huge numbers of login names, all of which are to be used for the same purpose.
Details of how to create a simple FTP folder for each pupil are given at the above address. Students will not have to worry about creating their own account - they can each use part of the teacher's one. This means there is a much lower chance of forgotten passwords if the same password can be used by all pupils.

Basic HTML
Worksheet 8B – Uploading by FTP

Student Name:________________________ **Date:**___________________

1. Web pages are stored on Internet servers. How can you upload your web site onto a server?

   ____

2. Why can't other people change your web site?

   ____

3. It is important to check that your code is correct before you upload your site because it is much more difficult to change it once it is uploaded.

   If you did notice a mistake after uploading your site, what would you need to do to correct it?

   ____

   ____

   ____

4. Browsers use HTTP (HyperText Transfer Protocol) to download information you want from web servers so that web pages can be displayed on your screen. FTP does the opposite.

   a) What does FTP stand for?__________________________________

   b) How is it different from HTTP? (Think of as many things as possible.)

   ____

   ____

   ____

5. At the moment, you have five HTML files in the **HTMLworksheet** folder. One of them needs to be renamed before the site will work properly on the Internet.

   a) Which file is it? ____

   b) What should you rename it to? ____________________________

Answers

2B – Writing HTML

4. <P> and </P>
5. <BODY> and </BODY>
6. The text is aligned to the left (by default in HTML)
8. b. (END) is incorrect
9. a. (SHIFT) will force reload the page in most browsers. (Note: CONTROL will work in some others)

3B – Graphics and Fonts

10. WIDTH=200 HEIGHT=300
11. Pixels
13. a. Landscape
    b. Portrait
    c. Portrait
    d. Landscape
16. Parameter 1: SIZE
    Value 1: 7
    Parameter 2: FACE
    Value 2: balloon (or "balloon")
19. arial (or "arial")
21. 7
23. <I>: Italic
    <U>: Underline(d)

4B – Colours and Hyperlinks

5. b. (Darker than before)
9. A thinking question, rather than an actual answer required
10. Norwich City Football Club
12. Bright blue/green - same as the preset colour, AQUA
14. a. black
    b. white

5B – Page Layout with Tables

1. <TR> and </TR>
2. <TD> and </TD>
9. C. (Because top row has merged columns with centred text, and bottom row contains Cell B and Cell C)
11. D. (Because top row has Cell A, Cell B (which is merged downwards) and Cell C. The bottom row add Cell D andd Cell E)

6B – Page Layout with Tables

1. Diagram with splash.html at the top, then homepage.html below it. Three other pages (charitynew.html, futureevents.html and howtohelp.html) in a horizontal line across the page below homepage.html.
9. Comment tags

10. <!-- this is a comment -->
11. The ALIGN parameter of the <TD> tag moves everything inside the cell to the LEFT, CENTER or RIGHT.
12. <TD> and </TD>
18. Nesting

8B – Uploading by FTP

1. Connect to the server using FTP and upload your files.
2. FTP is password-protected. There is no other way that you can change files on a server.
3. Several of these points: Correct the page on your own computer. Save the file. Connect to the Internet. Open an FTP client. Use it to delete the incorrect file on your web site. Replace the file with the one you just corrected. Disconnect from the Internet and close the FTP client and editing software.
4. a. File Transfer Protocol
   b. HTTP is read-only – you can download but not upload using HTTP – whereas FTP is read-write. FTP is password-protected, HTTP is not.
5. a. splash.html
   b. index.html - the first page in any web site is called index.html.

Basic HTML
Answer Sheet 2B – Writing HTML

Student Name:________________________ **Date:**__________________

4. ____

5. ____

6. ____

8. a) ☐ b) ☐ c) ☐ d) ☐

9. a) ☐ b) ☐ c) ☐ d) ☐

Basic HTML
Answer Sheet 3B – Graphics and Fonts

Student Name:______________________ **Date:**__________________

11.____

13. a) ☐ b) ☐ c) ☐ d) ☐

16. Parameter 1__________________________

Parameter 2__________________________

Value1_____________________________

Value 2_____________________________

19.____

21.____

23. `<I>`______________________________________

`<U>`______________________________________

Basic HTML
Answer Sheet 4B – Colours and Hyperlinks

Student Name:____________________________ **Date:______________________**

5. a) ☐ b) ☐

10. ____

12. ____

14. the background____

    the text____

Basic HTML
Answer Sheet 5B – Page Layout with Tables

Student Name:________________________ **Date:____________________**

1. ____

2. ____

9. ____

11. ____

Ordering Information

You can order online at
www.payne-gallway.co.uk

E-mail: orders@payne-gallway.co.uk

Other publications in this series

Title	**Publ.date**
Basic Word 2000-2002	Mar 2003
Basic Excel 2000-2002	Oct 2002
Basic PowerPoint 2000	Mar 2001
Basic PowerPoint 2002	May 2003
Basic HTML (2nd edition)	Mar 2003
Basic Internet (3rd edition)	Aug 2002
Basic Publisher 2000	Aug 2000
Basic Publisher 2002	Sep 2002
Basic Windows 2000/Me	Oct 2000
Basic Web Page Creation using Word 2000-2002	Jun 2003
Basic Access 2000-2002	Sep 2002
Basic Web Pages using Publisher 2002	Nov 2001
Basic Paint Shop Pro 8	Jan 2004
Basic Control with LOGO	May 2003
Further Word 2000-2002	Apr 2003
Further Access 2000-2002	Jan 2003
Further Excel 2000-2002	Jan 2003

Teachers' books to accompany most 'Basic' books and 'Further' books are available.